#GIRLBOSS

Sophia Amoruso

PORTFOLIO/PENGUIN
PUTNAM

PORTFOLIO / PENGUIN
G. P. PUTNAM'S SONS
Published by the Penguin Group
Penguin Group (USA) LLC
375 Hudson Street
New York, New York 10014

USA | Canada | UK | Ireland | Australia | New Zealand | India | South Africa | China
penguin.com
A Penguin Random House Company

First published by Portfolio / Penguin and G. P. Putnam's Sons, members of Penguin
Group (USA) LLC, 2014

Photographs courtesy of the author
Illustrations by Jo Ratcliffe

ISBN 9780399169274

Printed in the United States of America
13 15 17 19 20 18 16 14 12

Set in Avenir LT Pro
Designed by Alissa Rose Theodor

To our customers.

For without them I would never have become a #GIRLBOSS.

CONTENTS

#GIRLBOSS

THE only THING I SMOKE is MY

competition

The Chronology of a #GIRLBOSS

I'm bad, and that's good. I will never be good, and that's not bad. There's no one I'd rather be than me.

—Wreck-It Ralph

1984: I'm born in San Diego on Good Friday, which was also 4/20. Before you think this is some kind of omen, let me assure you that the only thing I smoke is my competition.

1989: I smear poop on the wall in kindergarten; perhaps my first true artistic expression.

1993: My fourth-grade teacher thinks something could be wrong with me. The list includes ADD and Tourette's syndrome.

1994: My dad takes me to Wal-Mart, where I ask a sales associate if they have "the Ren and Stimpy dolls that flatulate." This is evidence that I possess both a large vocabulary and a slightly twisted sense of humor.

1997: I fall in love with my first article of vintage clothing: a persimmon-red pair of disco pants. I secretly change into them in the bathroom of the roller rink.

1999: I land my first job, at a Subway. I get OCD on the BLT.

2000: I hate high school, and am sent to a psychiatrist who diagnoses me with depression and ADD. I try the white pills. I try the blue pills. I decide that if this is what it's going to take to like high school, forget it. I throw the pills away and decide to homeschool.

2001: My parents get divorced. I'm okay with it and take the opportunity to move out and be on my own. I choose an apartment in downtown Sacramento with a bunch of dude musicians. My room is a closet under the stairs, and my rent is $60 a month.

2002: I hitchhike up and down the West Coast, finally landing in the Pacific Northwest. I pursue a life of dumpster diving (do not knock a free bagel until you've tried one) and petty thievery.

2002: I sell my first thing online. It's a stolen book.

2003: I am detained for shoplifting. I quit cold turkey.

2005: I leave my boyfriend in Portland and move to San Francisco, where I am fired from a high-end shoe store.

2006: I get a hernia, which means I need to get a job to get health insurance. I find one checking IDs in the lobby of an art school. I have a lot of time to kill, so I dick around on the Internet and open up an eBay shop called Nasty Gal Vintage.

2014: I am the CEO of a $100-million-plus business with a fifty-thousand-square-foot office in Los Angeles, a distribution and fulfillment center in Kentucky, and three hundred and fifty employees.

(Insert the sound of a record screeching to a halt here.)

I'm leaving out some details here, obviously, but if I told you everything in the introduction, there'd be no need to read the rest of this book, and I want you to read the rest of this book. But it's true: In about eight years, I went from a broke, anarchist "freegan" dead set on smashing the system to a millionaire businesswoman who today is as at home in the boardroom as she is in the dressing room. I never intended to be a role model, but there are parts of my story, and the lessons I've learned from it, that I want to share.

In the same way that for the past seven years people have projected themselves into the looks I've sold through Nasty Gal, I want you to be able to use *#GIRLBOSS* to project yourself into an awesome life where you can do whatever you want. This book will teach you how to learn from your own mistakes and from other people's (like mine). It will teach you when to quit and when to ask for more. It will teach you to ask questions and take nothing at face value, to know when to follow the rules and when to rewrite them. It will help you to identify your weaknesses and play to your strengths. It will show you that there's a certain amount of irony to life. For example, I started an online business so I could work from home . . . alone. Now I speak to more people in one workday than I used to in an entire month. But I'm not complaining.

This book will not teach you how to get rich quick, break into the fashion industry, or start a business. It is neither a feminist manifesto nor a memoir. I don't want to spend too much time dwelling on what I've already done because there is still so much to do. This book won't teach you how to get dressed in the morning. That book is coming—but only after you tell all of your friends to buy this one.

While you're reading this, I have three pieces of advice that I want you to remember: Don't ever grow up. Don't become a bore. Don't ever let the Man get to you. Okay? Cool. Then let's do this.

#GIRLBOSS for life.

A #GIRLBOSS KNOWS WHEN TO THROW PUNCHES AND WHEN TO ROLL WITH THEM

1 So You Want to Be a #GIRLBOSS?

Life is short. Don't be lazy.

—Me

So you want to be a #GIRLBOSS? I'm going to start by telling you two things. First: That's great! You've already taken the first step toward an awesome life by simply wanting one. Second: That's the only step that's going to be easy. See, here's the thing about being a #GIRLBOSS—it's not easy. It takes a lot of hard work to get there, and then once you arrive, it takes even more hard work to stay there. But then, who's scared of hard work? I sure as hell am not, and I'm sure you aren't either. Or, if you are, I'm sure this book will change your mind so that by the end of the last chapter you'll be practically screaming, "Where is some work!?! I want some work and I want to do it *now!*"

A #GIRLBOSS is someone who's in charge of her own life. She gets what she wants because she works for it. As a #GIRLBOSS, you take control and accept responsibility. You're a fighter—you know when to throw punches and when to roll with them. Sometimes you break the rules, sometimes you follow them, but always on your own terms. You know where you're going, but can't do it without having some fun along the way. You value honesty over perfection. You ask questions. You take your life seriously, but you don't take yourself too seriously. You're going to take over the world, and change it in the process. You're a badass.

Why Should You Listen to Me?

Women make natural anarchists and revolutionaries.

—*Kim Gordon*

If there were rules to being a #GIRLBOSS—which there are not—one of them would be to question everything—including me. We're definitely starting off on the right foot here.

I am the founder, CEO, and creative director of Nasty Gal. I built this business on my own in just seven short years, and all before the age of thirty. I didn't come from money or prestigious schools, and I didn't have any adults telling me what to do along the way. I figured it out on my own. Nasty Gal has gotten a lot of press, but it's often spun like a fairy tale. Savvy ingénue with a rags-to-riches story? Check. Prince Charming? If we're talking about my investor, Danny Rimer of Index Ventures, then check. Lots of shoes? Check. And I don't mind—press is fine—but I'm wary of reinforcing the perception that all of this happened overnight, and that it happened *to* me. Don't get me wrong: I will be the first to admit that I have been fortunate in so many ways, but I must stress that none of this was an accident. It took years of living with dirty fingernails from digging through vintage, a few painful burns from steaming clothes, and many an aged Kleenex hiding in a coat pocket to get here.

Not too long ago, someone told me that I had an obligation to take Nasty Gal as far as I possibly could because I'm a role model for girls who want to do cool stuff with their own lives. I'm still not sure how to feel about that, because for most of my life I didn't even believe in the concept of role models. I don't want to be put on a pedestal. Anyway, I'm way too ADD to stay up there: I'd rather be making messes, and making history while I'm at it. I don't want you to look up, #GIRLBOSS, because all that looking up can keep you down. The energy you'll expend focusing on someone else's life is better spent working on your own. Just be your own idol.

I'm telling my story to remind you that the straight and narrow is not the only path to success. As you'll see in the rest of this book, I didn't earn many accolades growing up. I've been a dropout, a nomad, a thief, a shitty student, and a lazy employee. I was always in trouble as a kid. From punching my best friend in the stomach when she dropped my Play-Doh (I was four) to getting ratted out for lighting hairspray on fire at a family gathering (guilty), I was regularly the bad example. As a teen, I was angst on wheels, and as an adult, I'm essentially a young, half-Greek Larry David in heels—incapable of hiding discomfort, dissatisfaction, or doubt, inescapably myself and often honest to a fault.

I tried the obvious route of hourly jobs and community college, and it just never worked for me. I'd been told for so long that the path to success was paved with a series of boxes you checked off, starting with getting a degree and getting a job, and as I kept trying and failing at these, it sometimes seemed that I was destined for a life in the loser lane. But I always suspected that I was destined for, and that

I was capable of, something bigger. That something turned out to be Nasty Gal, but you know what? I didn't find Nasty Gal. I created it.

Abandon anything about your life and habits that might be holding you back. Learn to create your own opportunities. Know that there is no finish line; fortune favors action. Race balls-out toward the extraordinary life that you've always dreamed of, or still haven't had time to dream up. And prepare to have a hell of a lot of fun along the way.

This book is titled *#GIRLBOSS*.

Does that mean it's a feminist manifesto?

Oh God. I guess we have to talk about this.

#GIRLBOSS is a feminist book, and Nasty Gal is a feminist company in the sense that I encourage you, as a girl, to be who you want and do what you want. But I'm not here calling us "womyn" and blaming men for any of my struggles along the way.

I have never once in my life thought that being a girl was something that I had to overcome. My mom grew up doing the cooking and cleaning while her brothers got to enjoy their childhoods. In my mom's experience, being a girl was most definitely a disadvantage. Perhaps because both of my parents worked full-time, or because I had no siblings, I never witnessed this kind of favoritism. I know generations of women fought for the rights that I take for granted, and in other parts of the world a book like this would never see the light of day. I believe the best way to honor the past and future of women's rights is by getting shit done. Instead of sitting around and talking about how much I care, I'm going to kick ass and prove it.

My first reaction to almost everything in life has been "no." For me to fully appreciate things I must first reject them. Call it stubborn, it's the only way I can make something mine—to invite it into my world rather than have it fall into my lap. At seventeen, I chose hairy legs over high heels and had a hygiene regimen that could best be described as "crust punk." I wore men's clothes that I bought from Wal-Mart. On the rare occasion a guy opened a door for me, I'd refuse, taking insult, like "I can open my own doors, thank you very much!" And let's be honest, that's not really being a feminist, that's just being rude.

I now know that letting someone open a door for me doesn't make me any less independent. And when I put on makeup, I'm not doing it to pander to antiquated patriarchal ideals of feminine beauty. I'm doing it because it makes me feel good. That's the spirit of Nasty Gal: We want you to dress for yourself, and know that it's not shallow to put effort into how you look. I'm telling you that you don't have to choose between smart and sexy. You can have both. You are both.

Is 2014 a new era of feminism where we don't have to talk about it? I don't know, but I want to pretend that it is. I'm not going to lie—it's insulting to be praised for being a *woman* with *no college degree*. But then, I'm aware that this is also to my advantage: I can show up to a meeting and blow people away just by being my street-educated self. I, along with countless other #GIRLBOSSes who are profiled in this book, girls who are reading this book, and the girls who are yet to become a #GIRLBOSS will do it not by whining— but by fighting. You don't get taken seriously by asking someone to take you seriously. You've got to show up and own it. If this is a man's world, who cares? I'm still really glad to be a girl in it.

The Red String Theory

I entered adulthood believing that capitalism was a scam, but I've instead found that it's a kind of alchemy. You combine hard work, creativity, and self-determination, and things start to happen. And once you start to understand that alchemy, or even just recognize it, you can begin to see the world in a different way.

However, I think I always saw the world in a different way. My mom says that when I was five, I got a red string and ran across the playground with it trailing after me. All of the other kids asked what it was, and I told them that it was a kite. Soon everyone had red strings, and we all ran together, our kites high in the sky.

If I, and this book, have anything to prove, it's that when you believe in yourself, other people will believe in you, too.

"With my touch,
a plus-size anorak
became Comme Des
Garçons and ski pants
Balenciaga."

How I Became a #GIRLBOSS

The Early Days: Hernias, Haggling, and the Sad Bunny

So you've decided to step up to the plate and start an eBay business. You should first decide how much time you have to devote. I suggest you don't quit your day job (yet).

—*Starting an eBay Business For Dummies*

If I'm being totally honest here—and that's what I'm being here, totally honest—Nasty Gal started because I had a hernia. I was living in San Francisco, jobless, when I suddenly discovered that I had a hernia in my groin. I wore a lot of supertight pants at the time, and the hernia was visible even when I had clothes on, with a little bump sticking out like "boop." One time I even shaved off all my pubic hair, except for the hair that covered the bump. Clearly, I did not give a fuck. But all joking aside, I knew that the hernia was a medical condition that required treatment, and that to get treatment I would need health insurance. To get health insurance, I would need a job. A real one.

Where it all began: An art school lobby, a UFO haircut, and an Internet connection.

I found one checking IDs in the lobby of an art school and started to put in the ninety days that were required as a waiting period before the job's benefits kicked in. As you can probably imagine, checking IDs wasn't the most stimulating job, so I had a lot of time to fuck around on the Internet. MySpace ruled in those days (I went by the username WIG-WAM). At some point I started to notice that I was getting a lot of friend requests from eBay sellers aiming to promote their vintage stores to young girls like me.

After ninety days, I got health insurance, got my hernia fixed, and got the hell out of there. During my recovery period, I moved out of my place, and to both my and my mother's dismay, spent a month living at home. I had no income and no plan. But boy, did I have time. I remembered the friend requests I had accumulated from vintage sellers and thought, *Hell, I can do that!* I had the photography experience. I had cute friends to model. I wore exclusively vintage and knew the ropes. And I was an expert scavenger.

The first thing I did was buy a book: *Starting an eBay Business For Dummies*, which taught me how to set up my store. The first order of business was to choose a name. Many of the vintage shops already on eBay were so bohemian it hurt, with names like Lady in the Tall Grass Vintage or Spirit Moon Raven Sister Vintage. So the contrarian in me grabbed the keyboard and named my shop-to-be Nasty Gal Vintage, inspired by my favorite album by legendary funk singer and wild woman Betty Davis.

She's probably most well known because she was Miles

Davis's ex-wife, but it was her music (she had perhaps the best rhythm section around), her unapologetically sexy attitude, and her outspoken tongue that made me a fan. Performing in lingerie and fishnet stockings, her signature move being a high kick in the air with feet encased in platform shoes, she was the ultimate #GIRLBOSS. She had songs called "Your Mama Wants You Back," "Don't Call Her No Tramp," and "They Say I'm Different." She wrote her own music and lyrics and produced her own songs, which was almost unheard of for a female musician in the '70s. As mind-blowing as Betty Davis was, she was just too far ahead of her time to ever meet with mainstream success. I thought I was just picking a name for an eBay store, but it turned out that I was actually infusing the entire brand with not only my spirit, but the spirit of this incredible woman.

By the time I opened up the shop, vintage had long been a part of my life. I've always had a penchant for old things and the stories they tell. My grandfather ran a motel in West Sacramento, and my dad was one of seven kids who grew up maintaining the place. When I was a little kid, we went back to visit, and there was a junk room full of magic—an old Ouija board, '70s T-shirts with cap sleeves and crazy iron-on graphics, my aunt's old coin collection. It was just stuff that kids growing up in the '60s and '70s left behind, but I found it fascinating.

As a teenager, I preferred thrifted clothing to new, a preference that totally perplexed my mother. She endured countless trips to the local mall in a futile attempt to dress

Creep in polyester on
creep in polyester.

me, where I'd hold up a $50 top and inform her that it just
"wasn't worth it." Were there a Nasty Gal at the time, I think
I'd have found plenty of stuff for my mom to spend her
money on, but the mall was a boring place. The smattering
of stores screaming "normal" from their windows just did not
cut it for me, and the thought of paying to look like everyone
else seemed utterly ridiculous. Finally, we reached a compromise. Although she deemed thrift stores "smelly," she
agreed to wait outside while I shopped. However, this didn't
mean she always approved of my choices. I distinctly re-

member being humiliated in front of a friend when she demanded that I go back upstairs to change my shirt—not because she thought it was revealing or inappropriate in any way, but because she thought that my brown paisley polyester blouse was just plain ugly.

By the time I was in my twenties, vintage was almost all I wore. In San Francisco my friends and I picked a decade and stuck with it. We listened to old music, drove old cars, and wore old clothes. My decade was the '70s. I had long rock 'n' roll hair parted in the middle, with a uniform of my new eBay high-waisted polyester pants, platform shoes, and vintage halters.

With the new store I took thrifting to a whole new level. On Craigslist I found a theater company that was going out of business and negotiated a great deal for a carload of vintage. I threw some of my own pieces into that lot of wool capes and Gunne Sax dresses, and suddenly I had merchandise. I went to Target and bought some Rubbermaid containers, clothespins, a steamer, and a clothing rack, and got to work on my first round of auctions. I enlisted my mom, forming a primitive assembly line: I'd call out a garment's measurements, and my mom would write it down on a little scrap of paper and pin it onto the garment.

My first model was Emily, a gorgeous girl and my friend's girlfriend at the time. Covered in tattoos, with long hair and adorable bangs, she was an unusual choice—but she was a great one. I shot maybe ten of the items I'd accumulated, then plunked the description, measurements, and other information into eBay and waited out my ten-day auctions, answering the oh-so-exciting questions from my very first customers along the way. Each week I grew faster, smarter, and more aware of what women wanted. And each week my auctions did better and better. If it sold, cool—I'd instantly go find more things like it. If it didn't, I wouldn't touch anything like it with a ten-foot pole ever again. Shocking, but cute girls apparently do not want to wear "drug rugs," the beach-bum sweatshirts that some prefer to call baja hoodies. It was addicting; for an adrenaline freak like me, there was nothing like the instant gratification of watching my auctions go live.

I scoured Craigslist for estate sales, and then made a map, starting with whichever one sounded like the people who died were the oldest. I would show up at 6:00 A.M. and stand in line with people who were all at least twenty years my senior. When the doors opened, everyone else started putzing around for doilies, while I bolted straight for the closet to unearth vintage coats, mod minidresses, Halston-era disco gowns, and many a *Golden Girls* tracksuit. I'd hoard, haggle, pay, and leave. Also a regular at the local thrift stores, I waited for the employees to wheel shopping carts of freshly priced merchandise out from the back, and when they took an armload to hang up on the racks . . . pounce! I'd run over and check out what mysteries awaited. Once, I found two Chanel jackets in the same shopping cart. Flip, flip, flip—*Chanel jacket*—flip, flip, flip—*another one!* I paid $8 for each of those Chanel jackets. I listed each of them at a $9.99 starting bid and sold them for over $1,500. I didn't know what a "gross margin" was, but I knew I was on to something.

In retrospect I was probably the worst customer at the thrift store because not only was I sneaky, but I also haggled. "This sweater has a hole in it," I'd say after marching up to the counter. "Can I get ten percent off?" Even if it was only a matter of fifty cents, it was worth it to me. Every cent counted.

At age twenty-two, I returned to the suburbs, a place I had run screaming from just four years earlier. Space was at a premium in San Francisco, so I set up shop in Pleasant Hill, California, an hour away from my friends. I stayed in a pool house with no kitchen—I paid $500 a month and filled the place to the brim with vintage. I worked from my bed, which was covered with clothes and surrounded by packing materials. There was shit on top of shit: boxes balanced on top of a toaster oven on top of a mini-fridge like a game of household-object *Jenga*.

Every day, my topknot and I would drive to Starbucks and order a Venti Soy No Water No Foam Chai. Depending on the weather, it was either iced or hot, but there was about a five-year period where I drank at least one of these every single day. For food, I'd throw on a musty sweater with a $4.99 tag stapled to the front of it, forget that that was a weird thing to do, and go to Burger Road, my favorite place in town. I never thought much about the fact that I was spending $100 a month on Starbucks, or that I was missing out on anything by being so far removed from my life in the city. I was addicted to my business, and to watching it grow every day.

When I wasn't out sourcing new merchandise, I was at home, adding friends on MySpace. My outfit of choice was born out of my newfound lifestyle, devoid of any necessity to shower, get dressed, or look good. The Sad Bunny, as Gary, my boyfriend at the time called it, was a big, fluffy "mom" bathrobe that hung down to the floor. I sometimes topped it off with a pink towel on my head if I'd gotten the itch to shower that day—so if you're one of the sixty thousand girls I added as a MySpace friend back then, I'm sorry. Nasty Gal Vintage was run by a workaholic mutant dressed like the Easter Bunny.

I had friend-adding software, which was totally against MySpace's policy. I would look up, say, an it girl's friends and add only girls between certain ages in certain cities. Every ten new friends, I had to enter the CAPTCHA code to prove I was a real person and not a spamming computer. I was actually a little guilty of being both. When I'd exhausted one magazine, musician, brand, or it girl, I'd go on to another. The Sad Bunny and I were in the zone, entering CAPTCHA codes and watching our friend count rise as girls accepted. Soon I had tens of thousands of friends on MySpace, which I used to drive people to the eBay store. I did a MySpace bulletin and blog post for every single auction that went up on Nasty Gal Vintage. I didn't know it at the time, but what I was doing here included two keys to running a successful business: knowing your customer and knowing how to get free marketing.

I also responded to every single comment that anyone left on my page. It just seemed like the polite thing to do. Many companies were spending millions of dollars trying to nail social media, but I just went with my instincts and treated my customers like they were my friends. Even with no manager watching to give me a gold star, it was important to do my best. Who cares if a tree falls in a forest and no one hears it? The tree still falls. If you believe that what you're doing will have positive results, it will—even if it's not immediately obvious. When you hold yourself to the same standard in your work that you do as a friend, girlfriend, student, or otherwise, it pays off.

Every week, one full day was spent shooting in the driveway, with the garage's blue door as my backdrop. The night before was spent selecting an interesting mix of vintage, ensuring that no two similar items were listed at the same time. This way, my items weren't competing against one another, and I was able to maximize the potential of each. The models were cast via MySpace, and I paid them with a post-shoot trip to Burger Road. As I was not only the stylist, but the photographer as well, I developed a special talent for buttoning garments with one hand while holding my camera in the other.

When paying models with hamburgers didn't work, I'd get in front of the camera myself.

I styled the models like real girls who had stepped right into a fashion editorial shoot. With my touch, a plus-size an-orak became Comme des Garçons, and ski pants became Balenciaga. Silhouette was always the most important ele-ment in my photos. It was critical on eBay, because that was what stood out when potential customers were zooming through thumbnails, giving less than a microsecond's thought to each item. But the more attention I paid to fashion photography, the more I realized that silhouette is what makes anything successful. If the silhouette is flattering, it doesn't matter if the person wearing it doesn't have runway model proportions.

I remember perusing a vintage store in San Francisco when the girl working there confessed to me that to get outfit inspiration before going out on Fridays, she visited Nasty Gal Vintage. I started to realize that, though I'd never intended to do so, I was providing my customers with a styling service. Because I was styling every piece of clothing I was selling head to toe, from the hair down to the shoes, I was showing girls how to style themselves. And though you'll rarely hear me advocate giving anything away for free, this realization was one of the most profound and welcome ones I've had with the business. I always knew that Nasty Gal Vintage was about more than just selling stuff, but this proved it: What we were really doing was helping girls to look and feel awesome before they left the house.

The first time I wanted to play stylist, ceding control to another photographer, I made a friend for life in the process. When I came across Paul Trapani's website, he was already a successful freelance photographer shooting editorials for magazines. I figured it was a long shot, but his number was listed on his website, so I called him up. I was shocked when he answered and had actually heard of Nasty Gal Vintage— at this point, I was just a girl in a room with a few dozen crazed customers, hardly anything I'd expect someone like Paul to have heard of. What was more, he was willing to work for trade, using the shots for his portfolio if I booked the models, found the location, and styled everything to perfection.

Though I had a devoted eBay following and my auctions were starting to close at higher and higher prices, Nasty Gal Vintage was still a pretty small-beans operation. However, if the offer of a free hamburger wasn't enough to sway a potential model, the promise of a fun afternoon (and some shots of her looking gorgeous) usually was. I recruited Lisa, a beautiful five-foot-five brunette with doe eyes and pouty lips, to model, and we headed up to Port Costa. Port Costa is a remote little town in the East Bay that if one didn't know better, could seem like it was solely occupied by Hell's Angels. There's a bar called the Warehouse with four hundred beers and a stuffed polar bear, a motel, and that's about it. The motel was an old converted brothel, each room named after a working girl, like the Bertha Room or the Edna Room, and this was where we shot. The backdrop was a mix of awesome antique floral wallpaper and dumpy sofas from the '80s, and the light was hard, on-camera flash softened by the hazy sun filtering in through the window. I even made a cameo as a model in a couple of the shots, and we had a total blast.

Many people assume that working from home is like a vacation, where you get to do what you want when you want. This was not the case for me. The demands of eBay put me on the strictest schedule I'd ever endured. Because my auctions were timed, there were very real consequences for missing deadlines. The prime time for auctions to go live was

A photo Paul took of Lisa and me at our first Nasty Gal shoot in Port Costa in 2007.

Sunday evening. If mine went up late, that meant my customers, who were likely waiting to pounce on my latest batch of vintage gems, might end up disappointed, instead giving another seller their business. If I took too long to respond to a customer inquiry, she might get impatient, choosing to bid on something else. Shipping orders out late might result in negative feedback, and if I didn't steam and prep all the clothes the night before a shoot, there wouldn't be time to get through everything in one day.

After everything was shot, I became a machine. I spent an entire day editing photos. An amateur Photoshop user, I blurred out zits and cropped photos as fast as possible. I devised systems to increase my efficiency whenever and wherever. I uploaded all my photos to an FTP and used a template for my listings. My fingers were a carpal-tunnel whirlwind, typing out primitive HTML in equal form to a twelve-year-old hacker. When I wrote product descriptions, I exalted the details. I included styling tips in the copy, in case someone was considering bidding on a Betty White–type windbreaker but wasn't quite sure how to pull it off like MIA could. I included all of the details: shoulder-to-shoulder measurements, armpit to armpit, waist, hips, length. . . . I noted every flaw, and was always totally honest about the condition of everything.

Auction titles on eBay are more of a science than an art. Every auction title started with "VTG," for vintage, and then the rest was a word-salad mix of search terms and actual descriptions. "Babydoll" and "Peter Pan" were really big in 2007, with "hippie" and "boho" making an appearance now and again, then this eventually evolved into "architectural" and "avant-garde." To be honest, I'm glad I've forgotten most of these words and the taxonomy I used to arrange them. In those days I ate, slept, drank, and dreamt search terms. I'd wake up, the sheets and blankets a sweaty, tangled mess around me, practically shouting "'80s Sequined Cocktail Dress!" into the dark.

I loved shipping stuff. I got as OCD on the USPS as I did on the Subway BLT. I was a one-girl assembly line. I had a Rubbermaid bin to my right, a Rubbermaid bin to my left, and all of my shipping paraphernalia on my desk.

The bin to my right had all of the vintage items that had

just sold and needed to be shipped out. I'd grab an item and inspect it to make sure it was in good shape. I'd zip zippers, button buttons, and hook hooks, then fold it and slide it into a clear plastic bag that I sealed with a sticker. I'd print out a receipt and a Photoshop-hacked note reading "Thanks for shopping at Nasty Gal Vintage! We hope you love your new stuff as much as we do!"—even though "we" was just me. Then I'd put it in a box and slap a shipping label on. Only I didn't slap anything—I took a lot of pride in how carefully I affixed those labels. I had to assume that my customer was as particular and as concerned with aesthetics as I was. Anyway, the last thing I wanted was for her to think it was just one girl hacking away in a room by herself. . . .

By the age of twenty-three, life felt surreal. I remember a typical buying trip to LA, drinking canned beer in a friend's backyard. At that moment, I was watching my auctions close, totaling $2,500. I was making more in a week than I'd ever had in a month at my hourly jobs. While my mother was writing me long e-mails imploring me to return to community college, all I had to do was look at my burgeoning bank balance to think that maybe this time she had it wrong.

Sometimes there was so much demand for what I was selling that it actually became a pain in the ass. I sold a gauzy, ivory-colored drop-waist dress covered with silver and white beads, which looked like something an Olsen twin would have worn on the red carpet. For months after it sold, I received a barrage of sob stories from brides-to-be, begging and pleading with me to find them another dress identical to it. Sometimes they seemed convinced that I was holding out on them, but little did they know that I was no vintage archivist, but just a girl patiently going through every rack at the thrift store.

I took every item I sold seriously, obsessing to ensure my customers had a great experience. I took one of the Chanel jackets to the dry cleaner's while it was up for auction, and they managed to lose one of the rare-ass buttons. That jacket was $1,000 in my pocket, so you better believe I looked in, around, and under every one of their machines to find it. No dice. I called Chanel in Beverly Hills, and the person who picked up told me to send a button to New York, where Chanel would match it from the company's vintage archive. To do that, I had to cut another button off the jacket. Terrifying! But I did, and sent it off, where Chanel dated it 1988, matched the button, and sent them back. I had a professional sew them back on, and even though the girl who had bought it had to wait an extra week for her purchase, she was beyond stoked when she got it. I breathed a sigh of relief, and probably celebrated with a Starbucks chai.

You Can't Sit with Us: The eBay Clique

I completely dropped out of everything for two years. From the time I woke up until the time I went to sleep, eBay was my entire world. For every category on eBay, there is a seller forum. I wouldn't necessarily label everyone who sells goods on eBay as an entrepreneur. (Some of the women selling vintage on eBay have been peddling their 1940s aprons for a little too long.) When I came on the scene and started bidding wars over polyester dresses, these purists did nothing but complain. They were disgusted that I called pieces from the 1980s "vintage," arguing that nothing postdating the 1960s qualified. They also made endless fun of my models: "She's doing the bulimia pose again!" was a favorite about any photo where the model was slightly bent over, with hands on her waist in that iconic high-fashion pose.

Dealing vintage is like dealing drugs—you never reveal your source. It's natural that sellers are ultracompetitive. Hell, I thrive on competition! But eBay taught me that some people prefer to compete in ways I'd never imagined. While I was busy shooting, editing, and uploading my auctions, sneaky competitors trolled my listings to look for things to report. For example, it was against eBay policy to link to an outside website, social media or otherwise, from your listings. However, it was common practice among sellers to link to their MySpace pages—almost everyone did. But still, it sucked when you got caught. It just took one sneaky seller with too much time on her hands to report all of my auctions, and *bam*, all of my hard work for the entire week simply vanished. I had to redo everything manually, killing an entire day of an already packed week.

I became Internet "friends" with some other sellers, but on the whole, it was a pretty catty environment. Cutting my teeth on eBay was actually a pretty great way to toughen me up for the cutthroat world of business. Nasty Gal Vintage showed up, guns blazing, out of nowhere, and in no time it was one of the most successful stores in its category. What made me successful wasn't necessarily what I sold, but how I sold it. The photography and styling wasn't even that professional—it was usually a one-girl team of me, in a driveway—but it was still leagues ahead of my competition. Instead of spending my time trolling the forums and obsessing about what other sellers were doing, I focused on making my store as unique as possible. My customers responded— they were willing to pay more at Nasty Gal Vintage than they were at other stores. This, of course, did not go over well. It upset a lot of the other sellers that my stuff was going for so much, so the forums collectively decided that the only explanation for my high sales was that I was shill bidding, which is when someone creates a fake account to bid on their own auctions and force up the prices. I took it all in stride. Nasty Gal Vintage was growing by the day and I was busting ass to keep up, so there was no way I was going to waste precious hours engaging in Internet catfights. It seemed like a pointless waste of time, but it soon got too annoying to ignore.

Whoa Is Me: The Purple Flapper Dress Saga

Toward the end of my time on eBay in early 2008, I bought a flapper dress that had probably been a costume at one point. It was purple polyester and I styled it like a cute going-out dress. It sold for $400, and the girl who bought it was actually another eBay vintage seller, who wore it to her bachelorette party in Las Vegas.

But the eBay forums lit up. The forum trolls claimed that she and I were in cahoots, bidding on each other's stuff to drive up the prices, and that my dress wasn't even vintage. I had never claimed that this was a dress from the flapper era, and if the girl who bought it wasn't happy with it, I'd gladly have taken it back—but she loved the dress and felt she got what she paid for.

When noted fashion blogger Susie Bubble wrote about Nasty Gal Vintage in 2008, the comments section turned into a total catfight mostly related to what one commenter called "the purple flapper dress saga." Some people were defending me; others were leaving comments claiming that I had "risen to the top of the eBay heap based on FALSEHOODS and LIES." Finally, it frustrated Susie so much that she intervened. "I can't know everything and frankly . . . sometimes I just don't want to . . . ," she wrote. I stayed out of it, keeping my head down and doing my best as I've always done.

At this time, I was already planning to leave eBay because the business was growing so quickly and I was ready for the next step. With Nasty Gal Vintage, I had finally found something that I was good at *and* kept me engaged. I was beginning to see that it had potential far beyond anything that I had ever imagined, and to see that potential I'd have to go out on my own. However, this didn't make all the shit talking any easier to take. eBay was my whole world, and I looked up to a lot of those other sellers. Regardless, eBay made the choice for me. My account was suspended just as I was about to launch the website. The reason? Doing what I did best—getting free marketing. I was leaving the URL of my future website in the feedback area for my customers.

No More Auctions

Finally, after a year and a half, I had outgrown the pool house. I moved the business into a one-thousand-square-foot loft in an old shipyard in Benicia, California—even farther from all of my friends in the city. I bought the URL nastygalvintage .com, because at the time, nastygal.com was still registered to a porn site (sorry, moms!). I enlisted my middle school friend Cody, who was a developer. I did the graphic design and he did the programming. We picked out the e-commerce platform together, and he made it work. It was the first and last website I've ever designed.

When you leave eBay, you can't take your customer information with you. While I had none of my customers' e-mail addresses, I had my sixty thousand friends on MySpace to fall back on. When the Nasty Gal Vintage site launched on Friday the 13th of June 2008, everything sold out in the first day. Kelly Ripa's stylist called and asked if I had another one of those vintage jackets, but in an Extra Small? Um, no, I did not.

Soon after, I hired my first employee, Christina Ferrucci.

For the first year, I paid her more than I was paying myself. She haggled from $14 an hour to $16, both of which were more than I'd ever been paid, and in the back of my head, I was worried about whether I'd be able to keep her busy. But she was worth that, and more, and she was definitely busy. On her second week of work, she got so sick on her way in that she threw up in her car while driving and just kept right on, finally making her way to work. In she came, packed a bunch of orders, drove to the post office and shipped them, then went back home and crawled into bed. Christina is still with me today and is now Nasty Gal's buying director. If business is war, I always think that's the kind of #GIRLBOSS I want next to me in the trenches.

After over two years of selling exclusively vintage, I wanted to give our customer more of what she wanted. We were already good at curating ultra-memorable editorial vintage pieces for her, so why not curate new things as well? I was getting tired of the vintage schlep—selling out week after week, with no future of taking a vacation in sight.

Six months after launching the website, Christina and I attended our first trade show in Las Vegas. No one had heard of us, and we had never done this before. I approached Jeffrey Campbell's booth, knowing he was a brand we wanted to work with. I was instantly told no. One thing you should know about me is when I hear no, I rarely listen. It takes a special kind of stubbornness to succeed as an entrepreneur. And anyway, you don't get what you don't ask for. I marched back, opened up my smartphone, and showed

Jeffrey what he was missing out on nastygalvintage.com. Soon after, we were Jeffrey Campbell's newest online store and to this day we are one of his biggest customers. I also approached Sam Edelman, and when they were resistant, showed them the website and promised that we would make their brand cool. We did, and soon after we had sold $75,000 worth of their Zoe boot.

We started slowly. We purchased some stuff from a brand called Rojas; I remember it distinctly. Our first delivery was a red-and-black plaid trapeze dress with a shirt collar and button-down front. I shot it on Nida, my five-foot-nine Thai dream girl of a model who had been the star of the eBay store. A New Orleans refugee, she was a mere sixteen when she began modeling for me (I found her on MySpace, naturally), eventually graduating from high school while continuing to be paid in hamburgers and $20 bills. The dress sold out, and we reordered it.

We started buying units of six, testing the waters to see what sold and what didn't. If it sold, we learned. If it didn't sell, we learned. And we kept on learning. Six units became twelve, twelve became twenty-four, and our once exclusively vintage business became an online destination where the coolest girls could find not only vintage, but small designers at good prices, styled in a way no one had seen before. Nasty Gal was our customers' best-kept secret, but word got out—and on we grew. Sometimes Christina and I got confused and asked each other if an item had been taken down because it had suddenly disappeared from the site. On these occasions we spent a few minutes trying to figure out the system glitch before we finally realized that it had sold out almost immediately.

Though these terms are all too familiar to me now, I didn't know back then what "market research" or "direct to consumer" meant, or even that my customers constituted a "demographic." I just knew that talking to the girls who bought from me was important and always had been. When MySpace began its descent toward becoming a Justin Timberlake pet project, I, along with my customers, migrated to other social networks and kept the 24/7 conversation going. I thrived on it. My customers told me what they wanted, and I always knew that if I listened to them, we'd both do okay. We did better than okay, though. Together we were fucking amazing.

A year after moving into the shipyard, Nasty Gal had already outgrown the space. The company moved to Gilman Street, in Berkeley, a block from the legendary punk club, into a storefront next to a piano store. Our one thousand square feet had become seventeen hundred square feet and we had our own parking. Score! Here, we hired our first team: someone to ship orders and someone to write product descriptions. I called up my old friend Paul, hoping he'd join part-time as our first photographer in our storefront-cum-warehouse. Paul, always up for an adventure, accepted.

After Paul came Stacey, my friend of several years who was then moonlighting at the Christian Dior boutique in San

Francisco. She had impeccable taste and an iconic look: a rail-thin beauty with a mane of dark hair pouring over steep cheekbones. I trained Stacey in the styling tips and tricks of Nasty Gal, and it didn't hurt that she had once been a makeup artist for Chanel. She, along with our intern, Nick, brushed, blushed, buttoned, zipped, glossed, and dusted away; I focused on buying, social media, and running the business; Christina managed our small team. While many people would be happy with a manageable small business, there was nothing manageable about this. It was growing by the minute, it seemed, and we were constantly in need of more everything—people, inventory, and space, for starters.

In eight short months we had outgrown our Berkeley storefront. We needed a proper warehouse, and I found one in the neighboring city of Emeryville, the famous home of

Our first logo and my first business card.

Pixar. I had never thought I'd ever be taking on a seventy-five-hundred-square-foot space. I'd never worked in a warehouse and I had never negotiated such a hefty lease. I was both excited and terrified, and knew I needed more help than I currently had. The "champagne problem" of selling out of vintage faster than we could keep up with had begun happening with our designer stuff as well, which had by this point surpassed vintage in sales volume. We were growing 700 percent over the prior year, which is almost unheard of in retail. Customer e-mails came in faster than we could respond to them. Orders were packed with feverish delight, and my trusty '87 Volvo and I were schlepping to Los Angeles weekly to buy, buy, buy up a storm.

I had begun working with a consultant, Dana Fried, who (surprise!) I found online. He'd been the COO and CFO at Taryn Rose shoes, and had a lot of experience in running companies. Dana and I decided that I needed someone to run the guts of the business: fulfillment, finance, and human resources. We wrote a job description for a director of operations, but what I ended up getting was someone who was much more than that; we got someone who would help shape the future of Nasty Gal.

Typically, people with Frank's experience don't apply for jobs. I was shocked to receive a résumé from someone who had twenty years of experience in operations at Lands' End and had been COO of Nordstrom's online and catalog business. But Frank knew that Nasty Gal was on a tear, and also knew that type of fun is hard to come by. Frank had a lot of solutions. He told me about this thing called an "org chart," a tool companies use to map out the structure and hierarchy of their teams. Then, he told me about "departments." It was like we were inventing the wheel! First came a director of human resources. Then a controller. After that, a customer care manager, an inventory planner, and a manager of fulfillment. We got an IT guy. We got assistant buyers, and I got an assistant. We split up shipping and receiving, and created a returns department. Cody joined the team full time and became our e-commerce manager. We turned on the phones for the first time and had multiple lines and headsets—so official! No longer did our customers have to e-mail to reach us—they could just call! You are welcome, customers!

As we plotted and strategized, I was a sponge, soaking it all up. As the business grew, I grew, and the ambiguity that once terrified me became something I thrived on. I was still ADD, but found that running my own company meant that every single day, if not every hour, there was some sort of new challenge to tackle, a new problem to solve, and there was no time to linger on anything, let alone get bored. We hit our first $100,000 day, and I decided to celebrate: I rented a giant, horse-shaped bounce house and had it blown up in the warehouse. Send a few e-mails, bounce bounce bounce. Ship a few orders, bounce bounce bounce . . . It was pretty much the best day ever.

To everyone's surprise but mine, we outgrew our Emeryville warehouse in just one short year. By this time, I was getting used to the growth. It didn't make it any easier, but I could at least see around the corner, even if just a little. I stopped listening to the folks with experience—even Dana—because even they hadn't seen the magnitude of growth we were experiencing. In the fall of 2010, I once again started the search for more space. I was growing weary of my monthly and sometimes weekly trips to LA, where I crashed on my friend Kate's couch so much that I started to worry about wearing out my welcome. Nearly every showroom and designer we worked with was down there, and I was flying in to cast models we then flew up to shoot with us. I knew that I wanted to design and manufacture our own products, and that the Bay Area was a wasteland of creative talent who were just not right for us. With such conservative brands as Gap, Macy's, and Banana Republic as our neighbors, hiring was nearly impossible. For these reasons, I made the decision to move the company to Los Angeles.

Two months later, that is exactly what I did. I asked thirteen team members if they would relocate, and all but one said yes. Three and a half years later, they're almost all still here in LA, growing along with me and about three hundred and fifty others.

PORTRAIT OF A #GIRLBOSS:

Christina Ferrucci, Buying Director at Nasty Gal

I put myself through college working at a store in San Francisco and it was there that I realized I had a knack for curating clothing. After I graduated, I thought about fashion blogging among other things and came across a Craigslist post for an assistant at a place called Nasty Gal. I'd never heard of the brand and at the time my wardrobe was composed of daily deals from the Haight Street Goodwill, but I liked that it was vintage clothing and it spoke to me in a way that was unfamiliar but authentic. At the time I was beyond broke and I wasn't entirely sure what I wanted to do, and it seemed like being an assistant was temporary and I could leave at any time. Five years later I'm still here. I didn't set out on a charted career path; I chose to follow what I'm good at and what interests me.

At the beginning Nasty Gal was a one-woman show operating out of a small studio space. It was overwhelming to watch Sophia bounce from being behind the camera to styling a pair of pants to creating the graphics for an e-mail, but her energy was contagious. Sophia was very connected with the customers and held herself to a high standard to keep them engaged and satisfied. She put a lot of pressure on herself, and so I did, too. After a few weeks at Nasty Gal I was part of what quickly became a two-woman show.

Sophia and I learned about the business as we went along, most of which was through trial and error. If a style worked really well, we took note and tried to replicate that success. If a style was bad, it was dead to us. Pretty simple guidelines, but keeping it simple has always been part of the Nasty Gal DNA. Walking through our first trade show and saying the name Nasty Gal was an unforgettable experience and a life lesson in the power of persistence. We always said the name at least twice, because everyone asked us to repeat it. Then a vague smile or a bad joke would be followed up with Sophia's getting on her smartphone and showing them that it was a real website and it was cute. We made a lot of mistakes at that trade show about what we thought the customer wanted and what was right for the brand. Ultimately, we learned more than we would have if we hadn't taken those risks, and to this day I instill those takeaways in our buying team. I've learned to make really quick decisions that shape the future in a positive way. One talent that I bring to the table is my ability to insult the clothing. For example, "the colors of those pants look like hospital scrubs" or "the shape of that dress is for a toddler." This ability has served me well and has probably saved the customer from some questionable choices. Looking at the product is still my favorite part. I want to be part of creating the best shopping experience for our customer and I feel that Nasty Gal has the ability to do that better than anyone's ever done before.

Being a part of Nasty Gal's success has been surprising, exciting, and completely insane at times. As the first employee, I've worn many different hats (most at the same time). From being an assistant to going over HR benefits with new hires to being a buyer, customer care rep, or a manager to a shipping department full of dudes—you name it, I've done it. Now, as the buying director, I can say this has been a strange but rewarding career. When I applied for that Craigslist ad I stumbled on something that comes across once in a lifetime. It was meant to be.

"There are secret opportunities hidden inside every failure."

ALL ACTIONS ARE CREATIVE

3

Shitty Jobs Saved My Life

It was the straying that found
the path direct.

—*Austin Osman Spare*

The only good thing about being a child model was that I got to skip school.

I think I may hold some kind of record for Most Shitty Jobs Held Prior to Turning Eighteen. Or if not that, I'd most certainly win the Most Shitty Jobs That Lasted Two Weeks or Less Award. As a kid, I'd dabbled in employment: lemonade stands, a paper route, babysitting, and a brief stint as a child model that ended when I failed to muster the enthusiasm to jump up and down and shout "Pizza Pizza!" at a Little Caesars casting. My high school years were like speed dating, but for jobs. Maybe none of these shitty jobs really *saved* my life, but I do believe that my variety of short-lived failures, or as I prefer to call it, job promiscuity, made me an experienced young adult. When you have an attention span the length of an eyelash, it doesn't take long to learn what you like and what you don't. I generally have to throw a ton of shit at the wall before learning what sticks (and no, it is no longer literally shit). To the misfortune of all the employers I've left in my wake, it was well worth it.

Evidence of the low point otherwise known as Catholic school.

Before the tale of my litany of shitty jobs began, I attended ten schools in my twelve years of education. Because we moved, because our financial situation changed, because I hated it. By the time I was in third grade, my parents didn't know what to do with me—I got in trouble for being "off task," reading a dictionary in the back of the classroom. Some miracle qualified me to be placed in a rapid-learner program in third grade, which ended up being a joke—we read newspapers on the floor all day and my teacher "didn't believe in math." Obviously, this was not the solution, so I was then placed in Catholic school. And guess what? That didn't work either!

No matter where I went, I was an outsider (and generally led with poop humor, which didn't make me many friends). I got along as well with the cool kids as I did with the nerds. That spirit of forced tourism, along with my quickly learned survival mechanisms, eventually also made it easy to jump from job to job. Fortunately, the economy was in good shape when I began working at the age of fifteen, which allowed me to get a job, quit, and get hired again very easily. I was never disappointed when a particular job didn't work out, since I'd already lived an entire life feeling so far out of place that I'd given up hope that any one thing, place, person, or occupation could be my calling.

Misadventures in Job Promiscuity

I may not have gone where I intended to go, but I think I have ended up where I needed to be.

—*Douglas Adams*

This difficulty in "getting along" lasted throughout my entire youth. As a high school student, every time I heard the school bell ring, I told myself my life was over before it had even begun. When you're eating lunch with your über-liberal history teacher instead of hanging with friends, you know it's time to go. I managed to convince my parents to let me homeschool for the last part of my sophomore year. I had a teacher who came over once a month to dole out assignments, but most of my time was spent working. There was a Subway near our house, so I walked over, filled out an application, and became a Sandwich Artist. I wore the green polo shirt and visor with pride, working the day shift and conquering the lunch rush, despite not yet knowing what a lunch rush was.

Part of my job was to wear gloves and massage mayonnaise into the tuna. Sexy! I'd slap the tuna into a bowl and pour out half a gallon of mayonnaise, put gloves on, and massage the mayo in with my hands. Another favorite was the seafood, which arrived in a giant slab of perforated fake crab that I'd break apart with my fingers and go to town on.

I don't even remember why I quit, but the next job I got was working at a Borders bookstore. I really enjoyed this job. At the time, *Who Moved My Cheese?* was the book that everyone came in asking for. I didn't know what it was about, and I still don't. Sadly, my work at Borders did not involve mayo or rubber gloves, but working the information desk was a big step up, as I got to use my brain.

Borders put their staff through a pretty major training program, which, despite my anticorporate leanings at this point in life, I found highly valuable and still do. For example, they taught me to say "yes" instead of "sure"; or "let me check" instead of "I don't know" when I was helping customers. A very important tidbit about customer service: just apologize to people. Even if it's not your fault, they've been disappointed by the company you work for and it's your job to empathize with them. Though you may be paid minimum wage, to the customers you are the face of the entire company. It's this kind of accountability that gets people raises, promotions, and eventually careers.

As a teenager and into my early twenties, I thought that I would never embrace capitalism, much less be a public champion for it. I was certain that I'd live my years out trying to make a career as a photographer, getting by holding jobs because I had to, not because I wanted to. I'm not that cynical anymore. I've learned that it's typically the larger companies out there that provide the template for employees to chart a path for themselves and continue to develop in their respective fields as well as in their management skills. At Nasty Gal today, we have a little something we call "Our Philosophy" that's posted around the office. We employ an amazing Human Resources and Benefits team to ensure that our practices are fair and that our employees are well taken care of. Before Nasty Gal, I hardly knew what HR stood for (high rise, as in jeans? Or HR, the lead singer from Bad Brains?), and a philosophy was something that I would have fully rolled my eyes at. But when a company is on a trajectory as crazy as Nasty Gal's, and becomes as big as Nasty Gal, these kinds of things are more than just corporate mumbo jumbo—they're integral to having a positive company culture.

My stint at Borders, even though I liked it, only lasted

The fact that I quit my job at Borders in no way diminishes how much I learned from it.

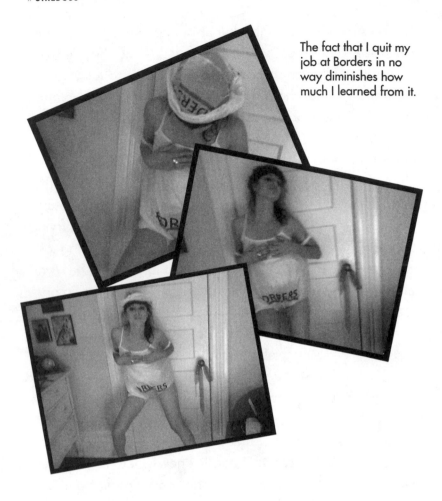

about six months. After that, I practiced more job promiscuity at the local factory outlet mall, working at a couple of different shoe stores (both specialized in orthopedic shoes) and at another bookstore. Then I worked at a dry cleaner's, where I sat alone, in the back, scrubbing ring-around-the collar out of men's shirts and separating them by starch level.

I worked at a restaurant for about a day, and that I really hated. I wasn't exactly a people person, and that's what working in a restaurant is: people, nonstop people. I wondered, if I was going to make the same amount of money no matter what I did, then what should I choose to do? To be a bumbling server (I say that only because I was a major bumbler), get stressed out over spilled milk, or sit here in this dimly lit Dexter shoes? I'd rather work at Dexter and read a book. Even though I always worked hard as an employee, all of these jobs still only used about 15 percent of my brain (max) and each job I loved eventually grew boring. It felt a bit like *Groundhog Day*—every day was the same, no matter how much I'd done the day before. And with no Bill Murray? No thanks. At this point in my litany of shitty jobs, I'd never reaped what I'd sown, and that, I eventually learned, is the only way I can stay engaged.

Fight the Boredom

To be, in a word, unborable. . . . It is the key to modern life. If you are immune to boredom, there is literally nothing you cannot accomplish.

—*David Foster Wallace*

This was the phase of my life where I chose jobs because they were really easy. The last job I had before Nasty Gal,

I was a campus safety host in the lobby of the Academy of Art University in San Francisco. I quite literally did nothing, and that was the entire reason I took the job. Hell no would I be making a difference or earning my keep! I wanted to be a cheaper version of a security guard, dick around on My-Space, and periodically yell, "Hey, you need to sign in!" As soon as my shift began, I was waiting for it to end. I realize how lame this sounds now. And guess what? It was lame. It makes me sad to remember how apathetic I was. I hope that I made some of these mistakes so that you, dear hardworking #GIRLBOSS in the making, won't have to.

What I know now is that nothing is universally boring—what's boring to you could be totally engaging to someone else. If you're bored and hating it, it's a big sign that you're most likely just in the wrong place. There are some folks who just straight up hate work, no matter what kind of work it is. This book just isn't for those people. Unless you're born the child of a billionaire, work is something we all have to do. So hell, make it something you enjoy, because bored is not a #GIRLBOSS's natural state. At all.

Unless you're powered by an ungodly amount of spite, it's pretty impossible to succeed while doing something that you genuinely hate. Personally, I am horrible at public relations. There's a whole art to PR that's being you on demand and saying the right thing at the right time, and that I've never mastered. A good publicist has to be capable of selling while still being genuine and building relationships. Kaitlyn, Nasty Gal's PR director, loves her job, and she's great at it. She's a total extrovert and loves people, so she thrives on being in constant contact with everyone all the time. I jokingly refer to the financial side of the business as "the boring stuff," but that's only because it's boring to me. Our CFO loves to look at graphs and spreadsheets and all sorts of acronyms that I am only just beginning to understand. That's fantastic, because if there weren't people who found finance or international logistics fascinating, none of us at Nasty Gal would have a job.

My biggest weakness as an employee (and also as a friend) was my incurable inability to be on time. Time may be the one thing in the world I can't negotiate, no matter how

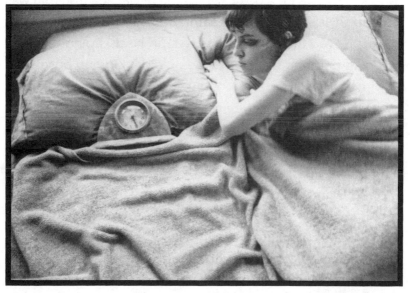

Using my love for photography to explore the oppressive nature of time.

hard I've tried. It plagues me to this day. I was always grumpy about the fact that I had to take twenty minutes out of my personal life to get to work, considering those twenty minutes were unpaid. To squeeze every last moment of "my" life (as I felt they owned me during work hours), I'd leave as late as possible for work, ensuring I was pretty much always late. Sometimes being late is unavoidable (aka shit happens), but being repeatedly, predictably late is a wonderful way to let your boss know that you just don't care about your job. No one wants to hire, or continue to employ, someone who blatantly doesn't care.

I finally found a job at a hydroponic plant store. We jammed out to A Tribe Called Quest while I balanced the pH levels of the water. I took care of a giant banana tree that was rooted in lava rock that resembled enlarged rabbit droppings. I loved that job. After that, I did landscaping, thinking it would be good exercise to be outside, lugging hoses and a wheelbarrow around an office complex. This lasted about two weeks. Go ahead, you can laugh and wonder what I was thinking, because seriously, what was I thinking? But no matter the job, the outcome was usually the same—I got bored and quit.

Yet when I started Nasty Gal, I found that I enjoyed work and thrived on challenges. My days passed by in a happy blur because I was too busy to look at the clock. This was very different from having nothing to do but count the minutes while someone who was no smarter than me dictated eight hours of my day. I've always had issues with following the rules, which has made Nasty Gal the only thing I'm capable of doing.

What all of these jobs taught me is that you have to be willing to tolerate some shit you don't like—at least for a while. This is what my parents' generation would call "character building," but I prefer to call it "#GIRLBOSS training." I didn't expect to love any of these jobs, but I learned a lot because I worked hard and grew to love things about them. Admittedly, some were way below anyone's intelligence level. But no matter what, I approached them with a sense of tourism and experimentation. Rather than being tied to how it all worked out, I felt like I was just going to see where things went. When you approach everything as if it's a big, fun experiment, then it's not that big of a deal if things don't work out. If the plan changes, that can be even better. There are secret opportunities hidden inside every failure, which I'll get into in another chapter, but start looking now—they are everywhere!

And the shitty jobs made the good ones more meaningful. Most people don't land their dream job right out of the gate, which means we all have to start somewhere. You'll appreciate your amazing career so much more when you look back at your not-so-amazing jobs in the past, and hopefully realize that you learned something from all of them. What I did before starting Nasty Gal gave me perspective and a diversity of experience, which for me was as important as everything that I've done since. It took me a while to recognize this, though, because I wanted a *Chutes* and *Ladders* experience with only ladders and no chutes. I was looking for something that would pay me to do nothing and still get ahead in life, and that, my friends, just does not exist (unless you're Paris Hilton, who I'm not sure is actually ahead in any way, especially when it comes to fashion).

I recently heard someone use the acronym "IWWIWW-WIWI," which stands for "I Want What I Want When and Where I Want It." One might call this the motto of my generation. We're Internet kids who have been spoiled by our desires being no more than a click away. We think fast, type fast, move fast, and expect everything else to happen just as fast. I'm guilty of it, too. I didn't have the patience to finish high school, or to go to college, or to wait for a career that would take a long time to develop. As an employer I see this often from new hires fresh out of college who expect to immediately get an awesome job that satisfies all of their super-pure creative urges and pays well. Hey, that's a great goal. But, like everything, you've got to work for what you want. I see so many résumés of people who've interned at 20 million amazing places. That's great, I'm glad that you were able to explore your interests and gain exposure, but if you've been interning for five years, to me it seems as though you don't *need* to work. I respect people who are willing to just roll up their sleeves and get the job done, even if it's a shitty one. Trust me, there ain't no shame in that game, and I can make one hell of a tuna sandwich to prove it.

School: It's Not My Jam

I was who I was in high school in accordance with the rules of conduct for a normal person, like obeying your mom and dad. Then I got out of high school and moved out of the house, and I just started, for lack of a better term, running free.

—Iggy Pop

By now, you've probably picked up on the fact that school and I didn't quite hit it off. Frankly, I have conflicted feelings about that. There have been many times that I wished I had the vision, patience, and discipline to have stuck with college for four years. I have a lot of respect for people who do. But school wasn't my jam, and the whole philosophy behind this book is that true success lies in knowing your weaknesses and playing to your strengths. In short, when you suck at something and don't want it anyway, cut your losses and move on. I sucked at being patient and sucked at seeing anything long term, which I have now outgrown. But if you're driven, patient, and want to go to school, I'll be the last one to tell you to do anything otherwise.

There were times when I hated school not because of the other kids, but the wacked-out adults I was stuck with. Remember the rapid-learner program teacher who didn't believe in math? Well, she lived across from the zoo and brought in raw owl pellets, dumping them on our desks for

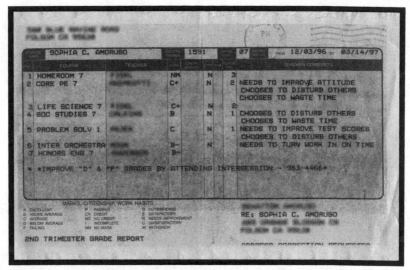

No caption needed: This report card says it all.

us to dissect. It smelled like barf because it actually was barf. I hated that teacher. In fourth grade, my Catholic school teacher sent me home with a note that detailed my daily transgressions. Ms. Curtis was convinced I was bonkers. My sins included getting up to drink from the water fountain too often, getting up to sharpen my pencils too many times, and taking too long on trips to the bathroom. My mom, completely exasperated at this point, said "We know you're not nuts . . . right?"

"Nope, I'm not nuts!" I said, so we negotiated. If I brought home a good note for five days in a row, then she'd take me to the Sanrio store. Soon enough, every Friday I was picking out Hello Kitty this and Kero Kero Keroppi that, my backpack filled to the brim with positive notes from my teacher.

In seventh grade, I asked my science teacher if I could stand on a chair while giving my presentation, because I was proud of it and wanted to make sure that everyone could see it. He said no. Hey, it's easier to ask for forgiveness than it is for permission: I took him literally and stood on a lab table instead.

As the years went on, I only felt more alienated. I went to high school in the suburbs, which was a sterile environment, and not in a good, non-owl-barf-having kind of way. All strip malls and outlet stores, there was little more to do than smoke weed by the river and sneak into apartment-complex hot tubs. High school was all bimbos and jocks, and popularity was a matter of how clean you could keep your sneakers. In those days, I wore flared jeans, platform Birkenstocks, and always a belt, usually one that was covered in spikes. I wore a do-rag, and my septum piercing was concealed inside my nose. *Obviously*, I was destined for a career in fashion.

The pure mechanics of the traditional school system were spirit crushing. I felt it was the Man's way of training America's youth to endure a lifetime repeating the behaviors taught in school, but in an office environment. I felt like a prisoner. I woke up at the same time every day and sat in the same chairs five days a week. I had no more autonomy than a Pavlovian dog. First-world problems, right?

My favorite teacher was Mr. Sharon, the one I ate lunch

Mr. Sharon, my favorite teacher and lunch buddy. He wrote poetry, *man*.

with on a nearly daily basis. He believed in me. He was vegetarian. He taught us U.S. history from the book *Lies My Teacher Told Me* and brought in bits of writing from anarchist Emma Goldman. I learned that Helen Keller was a Socialist! I was proud of my video project, which was a series of pans with Bad Religion's angst-ridden song "Infected" as the soundtrack. *Bam*, shot of the Nike factory outlet store. *Bam*, shot of money. *Bam*, shot of a graveyard.

But aside from Mr. Sharon's one-hour fart of freedom wafting through the jail bars, high school was a wasteland.

It was around this time that a psychiatrist diagnosed me with both depression and ADD. Though there was no doubt I was depressed, I refused to take the pills that he prescribed, instead throwing them away. I knew then that my utter misery and universal disinterest were not due to a chemical imbalance. This wasn't something that could just be medicated out of me—I just hated where I was.

It's unfortunate that school is so often regarded as a one-size-fits-all kind of deal. And if it doesn't fit, you're treated as if there is something wrong with you; so it is you, not the system, which is failing. Now, I'm not trying to give every slacker a free pass to cut class and head straight to Burger King, but I do think we should acknowledge that school isn't for everyone. So, #GIRLBOSS, if you suck at school, don't let it kill your spirit. It does not mean that you are stupid or worthless, or that you are never going to succeed at anything. It just means that your talents lie elsewhere, so take the opportunity to seek out what you are good at, and find a place where you can flourish. Once you do, you're going to kill it.

PORTRAIT OF A #GIRLBOSS:

Madeline Poole, MPNAILS.com (@MPnails)

When I was really young, before I knew what was up, I wanted to be a cleaning lady (because I loved making patterns on the rug with a vacuum) and a basketball player (because I loved the outfits) and I wanted to live in Connecticut and have a royal-purple foyer that I would call a "fo-yay" with a French accent. I wanted to be fabulous. Some things have changed but I'm still striving for fabulousness. I knew I didn't want to worry—I wanted a well-traveled, creatively inspired life where money was not my first concern.

I'd had countless jobs, usually creative but always low on the totem pole. I wrapped presents at a jewelry store, served snow cones, taught swimming lessons, cut bagels, worked at a coffee shop, and at a few restaurants—even Panera! I was breaducated. I restored posters, I catered, I nannied, I worked on an ice-cream truck, I sewed sequins on headbands, sewed tags on T-shirts, painted walls, murals, removed wallpaper, assisted a prop stylist, a food stylist, and some Devil Wears Prada—type fashion stylists.

My dad gave me a hard time, and all I could tell him was that I wanted to be an expert. Whatever I ended up specializing in, I would make sure to be the best at it. I was a hard worker, I always had been, and finally . . . I saw a lady painting a model's nails on the set of a photo shoot and thought, I would be really good at that!

I quit my various part-time jobs and enrolled in LA's cheapest beauty school. I was at my all-time most stressed and poor, sitting under fluorescent lighting, wearing a dust mask, watching a cheesy lady demonstrate airbrush makeup on a fake head. But I always knew it would work out.

Now I'm an on-set, freelance manicurist on fashion editorial and commercial photo shoots, I develop nail products, and I work on lots of creative projects that have anything to do with nails. In short, I'm an expert.

When I'm not working, I'm still working. I'm always observing, I'm taking photos of patterns and colors I see on the streets, I'm jotting down ideas, I'm meeting new people, connecting the dots, researching my craft, trying out new products, giving my friends manicures, working on my website, updating my social media accounts, working on my own products, on collaborative projects, putting together inspiration boards or sketching new ideas. I'm working on my craft and my business not because I feel obligated, but because I love it. I've always had to work hard because I had no other choice, but I always believed in myself.

I always knew I'd be a #GIRLBOSS.

"Discomfort was where I was most comfortable."

The STRAIGHT AND NARROW IS NOT the ONLY path to success

4

Shoplifting (and Hitchhiking) Saved My Life

We dumpstered, squatted, and shoplifted our lives back. Everything fell into place when we decided our lives were to be lived. Life serves the risk taker.

—*Evasion*

don't remember the first thing I stole. However, I do remember (with zero pride) that it happened a lot. At one point, someone tried to recruit me to shoplift an Apple MacBook for him, and that was when I realized that holy shit, I have a reputation as a thief. There are plenty of things I'd like to be known for (armpit farting, photography, my legendary dance moves), but being a fabulous shoplifter is not one of them.

I'm not proud of this phase of my life. And it's so far removed from who I am now that it sometimes seems surreal. Recently, I had a meeting with executives from Nordstrom, and then a few days later, a meeting with the CEO of Michael Kors. And the whole time, I'm sitting in this meeting, thinking, *Oh, my god, I stole a Michael Kors watch from Nordstrom when I was seventeen.* . . . These were my lost years, and there were dozens of times when I could have irreparably messed up my future. It is a miracle, and through no fault of my own, that I didn't.

On Anarchism, for a Sec

People have only as much liberty as they have the intelligence to want and the courage to take.

—*Emma Goldman*

For the latter half of my teen years, I was pretty lost. Though I knew who I was and always refused compromise, I had no clue what I wanted. I was willing to try almost anything, but my incessant desire to simultaneously reject everything created a challenging paradox. Another way to describe this attitude would be "immature."

When I was still living with my parents, I made the drive from Sacramento to the Anarchist Book Fair in San Francisco every year. As you can imagine, I listened to a lot of angry music in those days. When I was fifteen, I discovered Refused's album, *The Shape of Punk to Come*, and that turned me on to Guy Debord and the Situationists. I'd already been heavy into Emma Goldman, and was frequenting a Marxist study group in which my friends and I were the only people under forty. As I said before, as a teenager, I thought that life sucked and that my life—"oppressed" as I was by school and the suburbs—especially sucked. The ideals of anarchism were perfect for me. I believed that capitalism was the source of all greed, inequality, and destruction in the world. I thought that big corporations were running the world (which I now know they do) and by supporting them, I was condoning their evil ways (which is true, but a girl's gotta put gas in her car).

I wanted to live outside the capitalist structure, to live free and travel free, and to exist outside a nine-to-five lifestyle. I was like an old bearded hippie trapped in a teenage girl's body. I wanted to live spontaneously and to find myself in wild places, with wild people, and have wild times. Let me remind you, I was naïve enough to believe this was how I could live my life indefinitely. But thinking back now makes me scared for my former self the way any mother would be scared for her teenage daughter doing what I did.

At seventeen, before I even graduated high school, I moved out. My parents were in the midst of their divorce and too busy dismantling two decades of marriage to keep me safe any longer. I embarked on my dream of an adventurous life, trying on as many different experiences as I could. I was vegan. I was freegan. I hitchhiked to an Earth First! Rendezvous in the middle of the forest where I ate magic mushrooms and watched people set a pentagram made of sticks on fire. I refused to buy new wood; too angry with capitalism's

Do not knock a dumpstered bagel until you've tried one.

disregard for sustainability, I furnished my places with a mix of sidewalk freebies and lifted merch instead. I dumpster-dived at Krispy Kreme, dated a guy who lived in a tree house, and had hair upon my legs.

While this all may sound extreme, it didn't seem that way to me at the time. I'd felt like an outsider my entire life, in every school and at every job, and had finally thrown in the towel on finding anyplace that I completely belonged. Discomfort was where I was most comfortable.

Sun's Out, Thumbs Out

But if these years have taught me anything it is this: you can never run away. Not ever. The only way out is in.

—*Junot Díaz*

When I was seventeen, I decided to hitchhike to Olympia, Washington. Joanne, my travel companion I'd known for a total of twenty-four hours, and I stood on the shoulder of an on-ramp in Downtown Sacramento, holding up a cardboard sign. The first person who picked us up was a Russian guy named Yuri, who was driving a little Honda with a busted-out back window and a bashed-in steering column. In outlaw terms, the car was likely stolen. NBD, right? Nothing weird about that. I had a switchblade on my belt (it was for cutting apples!), and besides, we were invincible. Disclaimer: Please don't ever, ever do any of the stupid things that I talk about in this chapter.

We asked Yuri where he was headed, and started to get suspicious when he said West Sacramento, which we had already passed and was many miles behind us on the freeway. After some negotiation, he finally agreed to drop us off in Redding, which was at least on the way to where we were going. Then he threw in the deal breaker.

"For love?" he said.

"No!" I shrieked back, too grossed out to be scared. We

demanded that he let us out, and he started to apologize right away. But if the hot-wired car had somehow not tipped us off to the fact that he was a creepy dude, the "for love" deal breaker left little doubt. Yuri let us out at a gas station, still apologizing profusely in broken English, and this was how we found ourselves stuck outside a town called Zamora, backpacks in tow, and not another building in sight.

I looked around and saw two cars gassing up, but both were breeders (aka families), which any intelligent hitchhiker knew better than to approach. There was a big rig idling on the on-ramp, so figuring that this was our best option, I walked up to it and knocked on the cab.

A big guy named James answered the door, and informed us he was en route to Eugene. That seemed close enough to Olympia, and because we had no other option, we got in. James was from the South, and had a friend's son with him, as he was teaching the kid how, as he called it, to "drive truck." As we started up the highway, Joanne—who was a complete and total idiot—asked James if she could use his mobile phone, which in 2002 was a giant Nokia. He said sure, as long as she gave him a back rub, which she did! And of course, as soon as she was finished, he changed his mind. He told her that no, she couldn't use his phone, but he'd pay for her to use a pay phone. She got very upset as I sat there rolling my eyes, thinking, *You idiot, that's why you don't give strange men back rubs!* At this point, I had probably never touched another person's pubes, so there was no way at all I related to this freak I was traveling with.

By law, truckers have to pull over every certain number of hours to sleep—a law that keeps them from snorting speed and staying up for days on end. James's truck was huge, and had plastic, prisonlike bunk beds in the back. He pulled over to the side of the road, and quickly outlined the sleeping arrangements. "She's with him," he said, pointing at my idiot traveling companion and his friend, then at me: "And you're with me!" James had already told me that he was attracted to my hairy legs, which I thought was revolting because part of the reason I had hairy legs in the first place was to keep guys away from me.

"No way!" I said. "We'll share one, and you guys share one!"

"I ain't sleeping with no man." He chortled, making clear his disgust.

"Well, I'm not sharing a bed with you!" I responded, and told him that if necessary, I would sit on the floor and wait it out. This did not go over well with James, who made us decide: Either do what he said or get the fuck out.

For the second time, we found ourselves on the side of the highway with nothing but knives, backpacks, and a flashlight. It was three in the morning, and we were standing on the shoulder of the freeway, on the side of a mountain in southern Oregon, twenty miles south of the nearest exit. Joanne was really tan, like a homeless woman or someone from Maui. I don't even know how she got that tan, but that's an aside. I suggested that our safest bet was to throw our sleeping bags down in the forest until daybreak, but like the

idiot she was she refused, citing she was "afraid of animals."
Not afraid to give a giant freak a back rub, but afraid of getting
nuzzled by a baby deer, apparently. Our flashlights being the
only light available, we waved down another big rig, which
stopped about a hundred yards away because those things
are so goddamn heavy. We ran through the darkness to see
what surprise we might find behind door number three.

The next episode seemed simpler: just the driver and

Seattle, where I spent
almost as much time
cutting my own hair as I
did shoplifting. 2002.

his massive, drooling canine. The guy was a Bible-thumper who went on about Jesus and smacked his dog whenever it barked. He told us that his mom was a prostitute and that his brother burned a house down at age five. He was pretty cracked out, but for the first time all night, we were riding with someone who wasn't interested in Yuri's proverbial "love." Um, that was a relief. And the ride got better when the sun came up, as the driver let us get on his CB radio and harass the logging trucks, blasting them with insults like, "Hey loggers, do you know you're ruining the environment?" as we passed them on the highway.

This guy's trip ended in Eugene, and as we pulled into a truck stop, he got on his radio and found us a ride the rest of the way to Olympia. Our final chauffer was a very nice trucking dad who riffed about his wife and kids the whole way, dropping us safely in Olympia.

No Time for Crime

I think we are well advised to keep on nodding terms with the people we used to be, whether we find them attractive company or not.

—*Joan Didion*

At eighteen, I decided to move to Olympia, Washington, semi-permanently to establish residency so I could attend the Evergreen State College, an interdisciplinary school devoid of majors. No, seriously—you can major in Madonna. I still had no idea what I wanted to do with the rest of my life, but Evergreen's unconventionality made it seem like, just maybe, this was a school I could get along with. Because my political ethos at that time didn't really jibe with working for the Man, I started shoplifting—and shoplifting a lot—to support myself.

Here's some irony for you: The first thing that I ever sold online was stolen. At this point, I was palling around with full-time, bona fide anarchists. They were tree-sitters, activists, naturalists, hobos, feminists, radical publishers, thieves, scam artists, and one person who refused to accept gender, classifying him- or herself "z" instead of "he" or "she."

My friend Mack (an assumed name as I later found out, as he was a fugitive at the time) was a bit of a celebrity in this world. He'd written *Evasion*, a book that was a universal anthem for the underground society we operated in. The cover read "Homelessness, Unemployment, Poverty . . . If You're Not Having Fun You're Not Doing It Right." We were like Quentin Tarantino characters: a stylish duo with quick wits and grifters' tongues. We valued "social engineering" over socializing, preferring to spend our days tricking corporations into thinking we were just your average, paying customers. . . .

Books were an easy entry point for a novice shoplifter like me. Each time, I checked Amazon to see what the top ten bestsellers were, then made my way to a big corporate bookstore, waltzed up to the front table, grabbed a stack of that bestseller, and waltzed right back out with as many as I could carry. Why didn't I conceal my crime? Under Mack's tutelage, I learned that the more you tried to hide, the shadier you looked. The best thieves are so obvious that they don't even raise a brow, and with a stack of hardback thrillers under my arm, I was just another employee organizing the merch.

Once I got home, I listed the books on Amazon for ten cents less than everyone else, and they sold out overnight. Then I packed them up, shipped them out, and had a couple hundred bucks to pay my rent. In my mind at that time, I wasn't doing anything wrong because I was stealing from corporations and not from people.

#GIRLBOSS, this is where I call bullshit on myself. I *was* stealing from people. I took an inspiring quote from Chief Seattle ("But how can you buy or sell the sky? the land? [. . .] If we do not own the freshness of the air and the sparkle of the water, how can you buy them?") and twisted it to justify my own purposes. *Nobody really owns anything*, I thought. I had deep discussions about how I didn't believe in "property." It was the world—not my shoplifting—that was really messed up. In the words of another famous West Coast philosopher, Ice Cube, I needed to check myself before I wrecked myself. Unfortunately, it took a while before this happened.

I stole anything—expensive wine, spirulina, once even a rug that, when rolled up, was taller than I was. I was constantly adding new techniques to my repertoire. There was left-handing, where you paid for one small, cheap thing with your right hand while holding something more expensive in your left hand that you didn't pay for. No one's watching the cash registers for shoplifters, and if someone stopped you on your way out, you could just pretend to be a total bimbo:

"Oh, my God, what was I thinking? I'm so sorry; I wasn't paying attention at all," then hand whatever you were trying to steal right back. No cops, no fuss.

Some of my schemes were more elaborate, like one I ran on a major art-supply chain after Mack and I had learned that their computer systems weren't synced from store to store. Each time, I went in and got two sets of the most expensive oil pastels I could find. They usually ran about $100. I put one in my bag and then walked up to the register to pay cash for the other one. I was super-chatty while I was checking out, telling the person ringing me up that I was buying this for my mom's birthday, but was nervous that my sister was getting her the same thing. Mind you, I don't even have a sister, so I'm sure this one carved me out a special place in hell. Then I left with two pastel sets and one receipt.

Five minutes later I walked back in acting flustered and found the same person who'd just checked me out, to whom I explained that my sister finally called me back, and sure enough, she got Mom the same thing! When I was asked for my receipt, I acted baffled. "I don't know," I said. "I thought it was in the bag?" This store's policy was to refuse refunds without a receipt, but as I'd just been there and they remembered me, they always gave me back my $100 cash.

Then I left the store and headed straight to another location to return the second pastel set, this time with my receipt, for $100 in cold hard cash. Like I said: *a special place in hell.*

When I finally got caught, I was living in Portland, Oregon. I was at a large chain and had made my way around the store, filling my shopping cart until it was practically overflowing with stuff, having carefully picked the security sensors off each and every item before heading out the front door. The haul included a George Foreman grill, a basketball, fancy shower curtain rings, hair products, and tampons. I'm embarrassed to write this now and not because I'm the kind of person who's embarrassed by tampons, but because getting caught stealing a box of OB is probably what we would all agree was a low point. This time, my walkout technique finally failed. As I pushed my cart of goodies across the parking lot to my parked car, a guy came running up and trotted beside me.

"Hi," he said.

"Hi," I said back, my heart pounding as it dawned on me that he was a loss-prevention employee, in place specifically to catch people doing exactly what I was in the process of doing.

"Where are you going?"

"Oh, you know, just back to my car."

"Actually, no, you're not," he said, "You're going to come with me."

I panicked and pushed the shopping cart in front of him as I bolted to my car, but not before he grabbed my purse off my shoulder—and with it my entire wallet, complete with my driver's license. I made it out of the parking lot and all the way home as I watched my outlaw lifestyle fade quickly into the distance.

I was twenty years old and decided that a life of crime was not for me. In typical ballsy form, I drove back to the store, walked up to the customer service desk, and said, "I'd like to speak with your loss-prevention people. I just stole from you." It was humbling and humiliating and a huge wake-up call. Fortunately, I got off easy. The store tallied up what I had stolen and fined me, which saved me from actually getting in trouble with the law.

This part of my life was probably the ultimate low. I had an alcoholic boyfriend and I frequently found myself in trashy situations like this one. I thought to myself, *This kind of stuff doesn't happen to me.* Except that it did, and it was. I had always wanted to do something awesome, and instead I was just racking up a soap opera's worth of skanky experiences. Getting caught stealing was the straw that broke the getaway camel's back. I packed up my shit and drove my U-Haul-renting ass back to San Francisco, determined to do something legitimate and something brilliant. For a long time I kept the piece of paper that tallied up everything that had been in the shopping cart the day I got busted. It was a little reminder of how close I'd been to killing my inner #GIRLBOSS, and of how thankful I was that she lived.

Playing by the Rules.
Or, at Least, Some of Them

The only way to support a revolution is to make your own.

—*Abbie Hoffman*

After that, I stopped shoplifting cold turkey. It wasn't like I ran right out and got a job pouring concrete, but I told myself that there would be no more shortcuts, no circumventing the rules. I was experimenting with lifestyles and philosophies that were supposedly "sustainable," but as it turned out, they weren't sustainable for me. I eventually came to terms with the fact that living free doesn't always mean living well, and there are certain truths I had to reckon with. I was starting to realize that I liked and wanted nice things, and if stealing wasn't going to enable me to get them, I was going to have to try something almost too conventional for me—getting another job.

Being from the suburbs, I'd always equated comfort with ennui, and possessions with materialism, but I was beginning to learn that this wasn't necessarily the case. Living a comfortable life can allow you the psychic space needed to focus on other, often bigger, things, and when you treat your possessions as emblems of your hard work, they inherit a meaning that transcends the objects themselves. Adulthood was a lot more nuanced than I had imagined it to be and by age twenty-one, I was already outgrowing the life I had thought I wanted. I knew that someday I would be thirty, and imagined that rooting through trash in search of a free bagel would likely not be so cute anymore. You heard it from me first: That Syd Barrett haircut and yesterday's makeup won't be cute forever!

In my teens I saw the world in only black and white. Now I know that most things exist in a certain gray area. Though it took a while to get here, I now call this gray area home. I once believed that participating in a capitalist economy would be the death of me, but now realize that agonizing over the political implications of every move I make isn't exactly living.

Eventually, I got sick of listening to my friends whine about living in poverty while refusing to get a job. Compromise is just a part of life. We all, at some point, find ourselves either directly or indirectly supporting something we disagree with. There are ways to avoid this, but it generally includes eating roadkill and making tampons out of socks.

I was never one for accepting convention at face value, but through (plenty of) trial and error I have made working hard, being polite, and being honest a choice. It's as if I invented it! Rules surround all that we do, and no one, no matter how saintly she may seem, follows *all* of them. I choose to obey explicit rules—like, you know, paying for something before I leave the store—but the rules that society implies we follow, well, those are the rules I have the most fun breaking.

I always dragged my feet over the mundane, little things in life. They made life seem like a big hamster wheel. I hated watching my money disappear each month when I paid the bills. I hated cleaning and doing laundry and having to stop to put gas in the car. And oh God, I hated taking out the trash. But if and when your hard work pays off, these things start to suck less. The first time I had enough savings to put my bills on auto pay it was like winning the lottery. Renting a house in Los Angeles with a backyard and my own washing machine was like being in a really happy musical (no, literally, I twirled and cried tears of joy when I moved in). Having someone to help keep my house clean makes me feel like

I'm living in a fairy tale. Suddenly, you may find yourself with yesterday's underwear clean and folded and the noise of that squeaky hamster wheel fading into the background.

There's still a part of me that remains from my days of living beyond the law, and that's my desire to just mess with things. Life is unwritten, like a great big experiment. Why not see how long the red string of my imaginary kite can get? And why not let it whisk me up into the sky with it when my dreams start to become reality? For that, I think it's worth putting up with making some compromises, and even playing by (some of) the rules.

PORTRAIT OF A #GIRLBOSS:

Alexi Wasser, IMBOYCRAZY.com
(@imboycrazy)

I started my blog, I'm Boy Crazy, in 2008. It's a mix of funny self-help stuff and hyper-personal accounts of my love, life, sex, dating, and relationship experiences— all different things that convey the voice and plight of the modern single girl who wants a great life, thinks too much, and feels a lot of feelings. As a result of starting my site, I've sold several shows to Showtime, E!, and Amazon. I sell merchandise on my site, have a weekly call-in advice show, contribute to magazines, speak at schools, and basically serve as the big sis you've always wanted but never had.

I had no idea I'd end up doing what I'm doing now. I always knew I loved writing and making people laugh. But I went from saying "I want to be a writer" to "I wanna be a model" (I'm not super-ugly and I'm very tall, I swear!) or "I wanna be an actress." I did all those things, but writing continues to be what makes me happiest. Whether it's a book, movie, blog entry, or TV show, I have creative control and it's way cooler to be a writer than to be an actor saying the writer's words.

I learned at a young age that people were happy when I asked them about themselves, and I listened and retained the things they told me. I found that by sharing my personal experiences, like through my blog, we're not alone—that the most shameful, personal, specific things you're going through are actually universal. You can laugh about it. I want to make a contribution that matters, and I want to be as vulnerable and raw as possible so other people feel less alone. I want to make people happy or make them laugh—even if it's at my own expense.

I'm still trying to figure out how to balance work and a personal life. When you're freelance like I am, if you don't build structure for yourself, you feel like you always have to be working and it's exhausting. I think this is a constant struggle for every freelance career girl. Make a schedule for yourself that incorporates time for phone calls to catch up with your annoying family and friends, sex with your boyfriend, exercise, dinners, therapy, parties, texting, social networking, mani-pedis, shopping, and the work that's gonna get you paid to maintain the lifestyle you so desire! Create boundaries and structure! You have to be your own parent!

As for finding a guy who will support you on your #GIRLBOSS quest, I've accidentally dated variations of boneheads, such as the guy who appears secure and confident at the beginning of our relationship, but ends up being completely threatened by and uncomfortable with my personality, career, and how flirty or open my persona is. Another guy blatantly ignored what I do. He took no interest in it at all. I can only date a man I respect, am fascinated by, and consider interesting. If he can't do the same for me, we have a problem.

Figure out what you love doing and don't suck at, then try to figure out how to make a living doing that! Don't be scared. We're all going to die, it's just a question of when and how—so be brave! You will never regret trying to fulfill your dream! Don't get caught up in hanging out and drinking or partying. Celebrate when there's something to celebrate. Take pride in what you do. Don't do sloppy work. Be the best. Have something original and special to offer that makes people's lives better. Don't have sex with everyone in the world you work in. It's a small world. Good luck.

"When you treat your possesions as emblems of your hard work, they inherit a meaning that transcends the objects themselves."

5 Money Looks Better in the Bank Than on Your Feet

There is no dignity quite so impressive, and no independence quite so important, as living within your means.

—*Calvin Coolidge*

never set out to be rich. I had no idea my company was worth anything until venture capitalists started knocking on my door. "Your company is worth hundreds of millions of dollars and you own this much of it, and so now you yourself are worth this much." It was shocking how fast it all happened. Nasty Gal went from doing $150,000 a year to doing $150,000 a day, and now we do $150,000 over lunch. I think that part of the reason Nasty Gal has been so successful is because my goals were never financial ones. I believed in what I was doing, and fortunately other people believed in it as well. I cared as much about the process as I did about the results. No decision was too small. Whether it was the word choice in a product description or the expression on a model's face, I treated everything with the utmost care. At the time this was just because, like I said before, I'm the kind of person who pays attention to something as small as a crooked shipping label. In hindsight, I see that it's those small things that can make or break a business.

My adopted political ideals had let me approach money with an elevated level of distaste. I saw it as a materialistic pursuit for materialistic people, but what I have realized over time is that in many ways, money spells freedom. If you learn to control your finances, you won't find yourself stuck in jobs, places, or relationships that you hate just because you can't afford to go elsewhere. Learning how to manage your money is one of the most important things you'll ever do. Being in a good spot financially can open up so many doors. Being in a bad spot can slam them in your face. And being broke gets old, so start making smart decisions now to avoid paying for stupid ones later.

Credit Cards Blow

I wasn't always stealing stuff. Sometimes I went the conventional route when I wanted something; I went into a store and, you know, paid for it. And it was on one of these crazy such occasions that I managed to make a legitimate purchase and ruin my credit in one fell swoop.

I was nineteen and at the mall buying a bra at Victoria's Secret because while it's possible to dumpster-dive for food and trawl the Salvation Army for clothes, even a freegan knows to invest in new underwear. At the register, the salesperson asked me if I wanted to sign up for a Victoria's Secret card and I said yes. I thought I was signing up for a rewards program, where I'd earn points toward a free bra or something. What I failed to realize at that moment was that I had unknowingly been bestowed my very first credit card. Because I moved so much, I rarely had a steady address, causing bills to miss me as I jumped from state to state. By the time my $28 lingerie charge caught up with me, my credit was wrecked, and I had learned the hard way that you can ruin your credit in one seemingly responsible afternoon, but rebuilding it takes years.

When people write about Nasty Gal, the articles almost always note how I built the company with no debt, because that's a pretty unusual feat in the business world. And yes, once I finally got a job and started working for my money, I was extremely responsible with it. But what these stories usually leave out is that it wasn't by choice that I built the company debt-free. It simply wasn't an option, because no one would even give me a credit card, never mind a business loan. This was frustrating; however, it was also a blessing in disguise. As I had no financial cushion to support me while the business ramped up, I had to bust my ass and make it profitable from day one. In the end, this meant that I grew Nasty Gal to $28 million in revenue without borrowing a dime.

But I've also had to accept that credit is not something you can ignore. While I don't agree that the world should reward people for spending money they don't have, it happens to be the way things work. You can only ignore this fact for so long before it returns to bite you in the ass.

Like my A-cup bra did for me, it is the little things that can and will wreck your credit. As distasteful as it may seem when you're busy plotting to take over the world, it's equally important to stay on top of your bills. Parking tickets can end up costing you thousands of dollars and court dates. You could suddenly find the apartment of your dreams only to be denied because of that goddamned Target card you signed up for and forgot about while buying a mop, a sports bra, and mayonnaise. When you take care of the little things, you'll be pleasantly surprised to find out that the big things often happen much more easily.

Shared living situations are also a blueprint for financial

disaster, so try to spread the utility love among your room-mates rather than volunteering to have all the bills in your name. Better yet, if you're worried someone might not pull her weight, don't live with that person. Living in the party house is a blast until the party's over and you've got an $800 gas bill and your roommates—who are, like, your best friends and you guys are gonna know each other forever—are suddenly MIA.

Bills, sadly, are not an ignore-it-and-it-goes-away prob-lem. If you've been getting an overdue notice from the cable company every two weeks for the last three months, and all of a sudden it stops coming, that does not mean that they've gotten over you and moved on to someone else. Big compa-nies are like the mob—they never forget, they never give up, and they always get their money. Get them before they get you: Pay up, and pay on time.

Cash Is King

> Money is a guarantee that we may have what we want in the future. Though we need nothing at the moment it insures the possibility of satisfying a new desire when it arises.
>
> —Artistotle

When my parents pulled me out of Catholic school in fourth grade, I thought that they were doing so because they were the coolest parents in the world, rescuing me from the tortures of being misunderstood. When they filed for bankruptcy shortly thereafter, I realized the reason I wasn't going to Catholic school anymore wasn't because I didn't want to go, but because my parents couldn't afford for me to go. I vividly remember going with my mom and dad to the credit counselor's office and watching them slice their credit cards into a jar filled to the brim with the shards of other people's bad financial decisions.

From that point on, my dad preached a mantra of "Cash is king," and that has always stuck with me. It's so simple, yet so difficult for a lot of people to understand: Do not spend more money than you have. Sadly, doing just that is not only the norm for a lot of people, but also a signifier of success. Growing up in the suburbs, I saw it all the time: the flaunted backyard pool or new monster truck. These things often weren't a sign of what these people could afford, but only of what they could borrow.

For the obvious reasons detailed in the previous chapters, my parents cut me off financially when it became apparent that school and work weren't my top priorities. I now know that it was a tough decision for them to make—especially at a time when I wasn't inspiring confidence in my ability to take care of myself—and it was even tougher for me to take. I had friends who were supported by their parents and I was totally envious. It seemed unfair to me that some kids were able to do whatever they wanted while I spent my afternoons at a costume shop, helping "burners" find their goggles and stupid hats for Burning Man. However, forcing me to figure out how to provide for myself was probably one of the best things my parents ever did for me.

I come from a long line of hustlers. My dad has worked in home loans for as long as I've been alive, my mom sold houses before becoming a writer, and they have both worked entirely on commission since before I was born. In short, how much money they brought home was a direct result of how hard and how smart they worked. Sometimes we rented single-story houses; sometimes we owned two-story houses. My dad always said, "You're only as good as your next month," and in Nasty Gal's early days that was how I lived as well. No matter what, I had to get my auctions listed. Otherwise I was devoid of dinero.

When Nasty Gal first opened, I had little to no overhead aside from my sweat (daily), tears (regularly), and blood (sometimes vintage has sharp things hiding in it!). In 2010, after Nasty Gal moved off eBay and was a full-fledged business, I had almost $1 million cash in the bank. When sales spiked around the holiday season, I kept taking screenshots every time the account balance would go up, because I never knew if I'd see more money than that in one place, at one time, ever again. I wanted to remember what that many zeros looked like, forever.

Another big no-no is increasing your spending as soon as your income increases. I have always been careful to avoid this pitfall. For a long time I was so focused on growing the business that spending money on myself didn't even cross my mind. Even if I had wanted to drop $500 on a pair of shoes, I was just too busy. #GIRLBOSS, when your time spent making money is significantly greater than your time spent spending money, you will be amazed at how much you can save without even really thinking about it.

Though today I would prefer to look back and call myself practical and resourceful, the truth is that in the early days of the business, I was a total scrooge. If we absolutely needed something, I bought it. But if it was just nice to have, I didn't. When we finally went to IKEA and bought desks, it felt like a shopping spree to my inner anarchist (who was growing ever quieter as the years went by) who knew that we could have built desks with a free door and some milk crates from Craigslist. But as Nasty Gal hired up a storm and became a real business, we had to act like a real office.

In 2011 I took my first vacation since starting the company, and went to Hawaii by myself. It was heaven, and I extended my trip from a week to a week and a half. At the time, we were in the process of moving Nasty Gal from Emeryville to Los Angeles, and when I returned from Hawaii, in a state of semi-Nirvana after spending eleven days in paradise, I found out that someone had ordered brand-new Herman Miller Aeron chairs for the entire office. At that point, yes, IKEA desks were totally necessary. Aeron chairs, however, were not.

I happened to have a Herman Miller Aeron chair in my office. To me, it was a rite of passage. But I'd bought my chair with *my* money, not Nasty Gal's, and you wanna know where I got it? You guessed it—used, on Craigslist. There was no way that I was going to have interns rolling around on these things! It sent the wrong message to the company to preach frugality while balling out on twelve grand worth of chairs. You can't act like you've arrived when you're only just receiving the invitation.

We couldn't return the Aeron chairs, but after we were settled in our new LA offices, our poor office manager, Francis, spent six months selling them . . . on Craigslist.

In the eBay days, when vintage was selling for ten times what I paid for it, it felt like I was printing money. But instead of buying out the bar or heading to Prada, I started saving, investing every cent back into the business. As much as I liked the shoes I could afford, I liked having the money more.

Nasty Gal didn't have a budget until 2010 because we didn't need one. I always knew how much cash was in the bank, and designated chunks to spend on buying trips, ensuring there was always a healthy cushion for the business. As uneducated buyers, we bought much the same as anyone who had a small business would. "Okay, so we bought twelve of that dress last week and it sold out, so maybe this week, we'll buy twenty-four?" We trusted our instincts, and stuck to the two tenets of my philosophy: Sell things for more than you pay for them, and save more than you spend. Simple, yes, but that is the philosophy that ultimately led to a really big business.

One of the best books I've read was George S. Clason's *The Richest Man in Babylon*, which offers financial advice in a collection of parables. My ex-boyfriend read it, and it kicked him in the butt enough that he got himself out of debt and went on to save thousands of dollars. The average American only saves 6.5 percent of his or her income, which is barely keeping up with inflation. But you, dear #GIRLBOSS, should save 10 percent at the bare minimum. I know it's a lot easier to talk about saving money than it is to actually save it. Here's a tip: Treat your savings account like just another bill. It has to be paid every month, or there are consequences. If you have direct deposit, have a portion of your paycheck automatically diverted into a savings account. Once it's in there, forget about it. You never saw it anyway. It's an emergency fund only (and vacations are not emergencies).

If you're tempted to buy something, just imagine that those new shoes were actually made out of crisp $20 bills. Do those $20 bills look good getting dirty on the sidewalk? No, they do not. That's because money looks better in the bank than on your feet.

The Art of the Ask

To many people, talking about money is awkward. They think they have either too little or too much. As you now know, I'm pretty shameless, so from haggling the price of a sweater to negotiating with investors, talking about money doesn't bother me. Once, when looking for an apartment, a landlord insisted on keeping my nonrefundable credit-check fee even after I'd told him not to run my credit. I had called him five minutes after submitting my application to make sure of that. So I fought. On the phone, something came over me. My voice got low and threatening and I growled, "Fifty dollars means a lot more to me than it does to you, and I have alllll the time in the world to get it back." I meant it and he knew it, seeing that I was unemployed. And guess what? I got my money back.

A friend and I once stuck our thumbs out in a half-serious attempt to hitchhike on a Greyhound bus. Lo and behold, the bus stopped, the door opened, and we climbed on. Wet with rain, we were met with faces of equal disbelief among our fellow passengers. You don't get what you don't ask for.

You're in luck, #GIRLBOSS, as this mantra applies even better to money than it does to Greyhound buses. Some people may say that I was a horrible person for haggling at a thrift store, but I was just another person trying to get by. By the end of the week, those seemingly insignificant tiny discounts had made a material difference, and I could put the money I'd saved toward something else in the business.

If you're frustrated because you're not getting what you want, stop for a second: Have you actually flat-out asked for it? If you haven't, stop complaining. You can't expect the world to read your mind. You have to put it out there, and sometimes putting it out there is as simple as just saying, "Hey, can I have that?"

That being said, if you don't like talking about money, I get it. There are ways to make the whole thing less traumatic. The first piece of advice I can give you is to learn to separate your money from your emotions as much as you possibly can. Whether someone is asking you for money, you're asking someone else, or you're contemplating a significant purchase, approaching financial decisions as calmly and as rationally as possible will make everything a whole lot easier.

It also quite literally pays to be as unemotional as possible when you're asking for a raise. First, be really honest with yourself and make sure that you deserve the raise that you're asking for. You do not automatically deserve a raise just because you've been somewhere for a certain amount of time. But if you can articulate the reasons why you deserve a pay increase, then schedule time to meet with your boss and let her know in advance what you want to talk about. This can be as simple as "I'd like to schedule some time with you to talk about my salary. Is it okay if we put something on the calendar?" Talk to your boss about this in person. Hitting him up on Gchat is not appropriate. If your company does regular yearly reviews, that can also be your chance to talk about money.

When you do meet to discuss it, skip the personal sob stories. The only factor that affects your chance of getting a raise is whether or not you've earned it. It doesn't matter if your car broke down or that your landlord's raising your rent. Those facts are not your boss's problem. All she needs to know is that you're kicking ass, like a #GIRLBOSS should.

Put That Money to Work

While I still don't blow my money, I am now comfortable with buying expensive stuff. It is natural, at some point, to realize that it's worth it to spend a little extra (if you can afford it) to get something that's just right. This is true when it comes to buying clothes and it is true when hiring employees— sometimes it pays to spend a little more than you bargained for on real quality.

Spend money because it's an investment in your own well-being, not because you're bored and have nothing else to do. Don't get all Versace-Versace-Versace and buy things just because you can. Luxury can be a great experience, and the things around you should represent the life that you've made for yourself, as long as you are taking the time to appreciate those items. I bought silverware recently, and when I was eating my yogurt this morning, I couldn't help but think, *This spoon is serious!*

Don't live like a CEO when you're still a sandwich artist. The first car I bought after the Volvo wasn't a Porsche—it was a used Nissan Murano. I loved this car. I put half down (around $10,000), financed the rest with an 11 percent interest rate (my first loan!), and was so excited about the horrible deal I had just gotten that I hugged the car salesman when he handed me the keys. I paid it off in full within the next year.

Last year I decided it was time to upgrade. One great thing about Los Angeles is that you can get away with being flamboyant with little consequence. It's a car-centric city, where driving can be rush-hour hell or a hedonistic romp. Cruising down Sunset Boulevard with the Cramps blasting and palm trees silhouetted by the neon signs of strip clubs can sometimes repair the worst of my moods. When I went to buy the Porsche, I was ready to splurge. But me being me, I wanted to again put half down.

The dealership, however, put a kink in my well-laid plans for a financially responsible splurge. They wouldn't give me a loan or a lease. Who would have guessed that Porsche had stingier financing than Nissan? And, as it turned out, even though I was now running my own company and had enough money to put down a hefty deposit, my credit was still only mediocre. It was a WTF moment that drove home to me how screwy the credit system is. I was reminded again that the common way is not always the best way. Therefore, I paid cash for that Porsche. A #GIRLBOSS has gotta do what a #GIRLBOSS has gotta do.

This time, when I got my keys, nobody got a hug. And no, it wasn't because I was bitter about the financing. It's that buying the Porsche, in all of its German-engineered perfection, just wasn't as special. Nothing will ever compare to the first time I bought myself a car, because it simply can't be done again.

Hocus-pocus: The Power of Magical Thinking

Do what thou wilt shall be the whole of the law.

—Aleister Crowley

I hate the concept of luck, especially when people try to apply it to me. Yes, it's true: Hundreds of thousands of businesses fail. Mine succeeded. Was that all just because I "got lucky"? I don't really think so.

What I hate about luck is that it implies being devoid of responsibility. It implies that you can do nothing and then step into success as easily as stepping into a pile of dog poop on the sidewalk. It implies that success is something given to a knighted and often undeserving few. Luck tells us that we don't control our own fate, and that our path to success or failure is written by someone, or something, entirely outside ourselves. Luck lets us believe that whatever happens, whether good or bad, it's not to our credit or our fault. That is why I don't buy luck.

But I do buy magic.

I'm a member of the Magic Castle, which is a private magician's club housed in an old Victorian mansion in the Hollywood Hills. Its floors are carpeted, its waiters tuxedoed, and its drinks strong. Quite often, my boyfriend and I are the youngest ones there, but in my mind, there is no better or more glamorous place to spend a Saturday night, all dressed up with a champagne cocktail in hand, watching an aging showgirl do a tap-dance shuffle on stage while a man works the crowd with a dove in one pocket and a few card tricks in the other.

There's that kind of magic, for sure. But there's also the everyday kind of magic that we make for ourselves. And that's really not magic at all. It's just recognizing the fact that we control our thoughts and our thoughts control our lives. This is an extremely simple, totally straightforward concept, but for a lot of people, it's so alien that it might as well be magic. Chances are that you know someone who is really negative. You know the type: always complaining, getting fired, having her car broken into, his girlfriend is cheating on him. These people are convinced that life is shit . . . and so it is. It's the age-old concept of like attracts like, or the law of attraction. You get back what you put out, so you might as well think positively, focus on visualizing what you want instead of getting distracted by what you don't want, and send the universe your good intentions so that it can send them right back.

The success of Nasty Gal has been a wild and fast ride, and I'm not going to lie: There were times when that ride has been absolutely terrifying. For about the first year after the business really started to take off, I felt like a lamb being led to slaughter. We were hiring like crazy and getting tons of attention from press and starting to get noticed by investors. Every day I got up, went to work, and got hit in the face with something that I never could have predicted from a business that I'd originally started so I wouldn't have to talk to people. I went from doing small tasks with measurable results (selling more clothes!) to abstractions like going on *E! News* to talk about what's hot, or speaking at a conference. I didn't want to talk about my job—I wanted to do my job. But then talking about my job became my job. Even worse, people expected me to be a certain way just because I'd accomplished something. A sizeable part of me resented the fact that I had to choose my words carefully.

I often wondered, *Was this a choice?* Because it sure as hell doesn't always feel like it. But I did choose it—even if growing a huge business was never my singular goal, every small choice that I made along the way was something that contributed to where I am now. Every time I got up in the morning instead of saying "screw it" and sleeping in, every time I spent a few extra minutes on a product description to make it perfect, I was choosing my fate and sowing the seeds of my future. It's really hard to chart the path that led here, but it happened, and I did it.

In my book (and this is my book!) magical thinking is the alchemy that you can use to visualize and project yourself into the professional and personal life that you want. I'm not talking about stuff like *The Secret* self-help book, which basically tells you to tape a picture of a car to the wall and then sit on the couch and wait for someone to drop it off in your driveway. I am talking about visualization that works when we actually get off our asses and do stuff. How totally crazy is that? Each time you make a good decision or do something nice or take care of yourself; each time you show up to work and work hard and do your best at everything you can do, you're planting seeds for a life that you can only hope will grow beyond your wildest dreams. Take care of the little things—even the little things that you hate—and treat them as promises to your own future. Soon you'll see that fortune favors the bold who get shit done.

Chaos Magic

Those who don't believe in magic will never find it.

—*Roald Dahl*

Chaos magic is the idea that a particular set of beliefs serves as an active force in the world. In other words, we choose what and how we believe, and our beliefs are tools that we then use to make things happen . . . or not. Though this comes from a school of magical thought, it actually seems really practical and "no duh" to me. It all goes back to the red string of my imaginary kite—if you believe something, other people will believe it, too. You can't convince someone else—whether it's a potential employer, a loan officer at the car dealership, or someone you've been crushing on—that you're amazing and terrific if you don't actually think you are. This isn't the false confidence that comes from getting a bunch of "likes" on your Instagram selfies, but a deep-down, unshakeable self-confidence that persists even when things aren't going all that great.

A big practice in chaos magic is the use of sigils, which are abstract words or symbols you create and embed with your wishes. To create a sigil, start by writing out your desire in a single word, a couple of words, or a short sentence. Then remove all the duplicate letters, then all the vowels— basically, you can do whatever you want here—until you're left with a bunch of lines that you can combine into one symbol. Then you put the piece of paper in a book, in your wallet, or some other place where it won't get lost, and just forget about it.

The real "magic" of sigils is that you're only forgetting about it on the surface level. Taking the time to think about what you really want and doing something about it, even if it's just drawing some lines on a piece of paper, embeds these wishes into your subconscious, and then your subconscious makes it happen, even when the conscious part of your brain is busy doing something else.

I treat my Internet passwords as modern-day sigils, embedding them with wishes or promises to me, or even financial goals for the company. (Hey, I never made any claims to be normal here.) That way, every time I go to log in anywhere, I'm subtly reminding myself of what I'm working for. This kind of intention setting has worked for me. Dozens of times a day, as I tap out a few strokes on the keyboard, I'm reminding myself of the bigger picture. This ensures that when I'm bogged down with day-to-day bureaucracy and details, I don't lose sight of what I really want.

I'm not trying to say that this kind of intention setting will always work, because you can't just type "abajilliondollars" whenever you log in to Facebook and all of a sudden become Warren Buffett. It is, though, a heretic's version of kneeling by your bed and saying a prayer every night. It's intention setting. It doesn't have to be as hard and fast as saying "I want a job at a fashion company," but it can be something like "I want a creative job" or "I want to have fun at work." Keep reminding yourself over and over that this is what you want, and you'll soon find that the more you know what you want, the less you're willing to put up with what you don't. One of the best things about life—a reason not to go blindly after one goal and one goal only—is that sometimes it will take you to something that is way cooler than anything you would have consciously set out to do in the first place. I never had one particular goal or dream that I was working toward; all I knew was that I wanted to do something awesome, and was open to whatever shape or form this awesomeness took. I wanted to be a photographer; I wanted to go to art school; I wanted to play in a band; and when I started the eBay store, all of this came in handy even though I would never have associated these things.

My interest in photography gave me an advantage over other sellers who didn't care about lighting or composition. My days of being the tardy employee at the record store gave me a cultural and musical understanding that was more unique than if I'd just listened to garbage-y pop on the radio my entire life. None of these were things I ever expected to add up to something called a brand, but they contributed to all the ways in which Nasty Gal is just a little off and a little surprising. All of that flailing about, trying new things and finding out that I liked some of them and hated others, ended up amalgamating into something very real and very meaningful, and in the end, made me capable of providing a life for myself.

While I truly believe that you must have intentions to fulfill your dreams, I also think you have to leave room for the universe to have its way and play around a bit. Don't get so focused on one particular opportunity that you're blind to other ones that come up. If you think about one thing, and talk about it all the time, you're being too obsessive. You might ruin it. If you let yourself meander a bit, then the right things and the right people fall into place. Some things are worth fighting for—don't get me wrong, I'm definitely a fighter—but I really think that what is right should be easy. My dad has always said that the definition of crazy is doing the same thing over and over and expecting different results, and it's so true. If something's not working out, but you keep hammering at it in the exact same way, go after something else for a while. That's not giving up, that's just letting the universe have its way.

Treat Your Thoughts Like Your Dollar Bills: Don't Waste 'Em

Though I believe in magic, I'm not hippy-dippy and I generally abhor people who are. I remember I had a hippie friend once who whispered, "The cat can sense the stillness in my soul," and all I could think was, *The cat is really going to sense it if I barf because you sound so self-important.* That said, if you approach everything in your life with a certain degree of intention, you can affect the outcome. At the absolute minimum, you will affect how you feel about the outcome and that is ultimately what matters the most. If I am in a shitty mood while making dinner, the food is going to taste like crap. But if I'm happy while I'm cooking, then dinner is going to be absolutely fantastic.

I also think you can end up ignoring, and even losing, the positive things in your life by focusing too much on the negative. That's a huge drain, as well as a waste of time. When you think about people, you give them power. My ex-boyfriend Gary taught me this lesson when we first started dating. This was the heyday of MySpace, when you could always see who was commenting on whose page, so I knew way too much about this one girl—or woman, because she was *waayyy* older than me—whom he had once hooked up with and who was still lurking around. She was my favorite horrible thing to talk about, and I brought her up a little too often. For obvious reasons this would piss him off. When he finally got fed up with the subject, he said, "I don't think about her, and I don't want to think about her, but when you bring her up, I have to think about her and it makes me uncomfortable. Why are you doing that to me? Why are you doing it to yourself?"

Turns out he had a point.

Flash back to Halloween several years ago; he and I were at the Deco Lounge in San Francisco. He was dressed as a monk and was wearing this hundred-year-old Masonic robe—which, let's face it, was basically a giant black dress with a skull on it. And I was dressed as a blaxploitation character, wearing a halter disco gown and a giant Afro wig. Not the most politically correct choice, I realize, but as I've said before, this was San Francisco and you picked a decade and stuck with it, even in costume.

As we were getting ready to go out that night, I mentioned this woman's name again, wondering if we would run into her. It was unlikely, as she lived in LA at the time, but she was known to lurk up north. As soon as we walked into the bar, there she was. She saw Gary, made a beeline for him, and began to whisper in his ear as soon as she was close enough. She totally ignored me, even though I was only inches away and holding his hand.

"Hi," I said, interjecting myself into her whisper fest with an introduction. "I'm Sophia." I mustered every molecule of inner goodwill to put a smile on my face.

But she just turned and looked at me with a snarl. "Oh, are you his ex-girlfriend?"

"No, I'm his girlfriend," I said, no longer caring at all about trying to be nice. "So, what are you even doing at this bar at your age, anyway?" And that, dear #GIRLBOSS, was what started the only fight I've ever been in.

She pulled my Afro off, I punched her in the nose, and Gary dove in between us, pulling her off me as we went at it on the Deco Lounge floor. Though I can laugh at it now—the absurdity of costumes and wigs and punches and a man in a dress breaking it up—it was a miserable Halloween and a miserable night. During the miserable cab ride home, I realized that I'd put so much energy into thinking about what I didn't want to happen that I'd caused that exact thing to happen.

I conjured that bitch.

I have also had to learn to rein in my negative thoughts

when it comes to business competition. Around the same time that I launched the Nasty Gal website, I had become pretty good friends with another girl who ran a vintage eBay shop. We talked shop, but in a way that I always assumed was friendly banter between two people who had a lot in common, and not sharing state secrets. A year after I left eBay and set Nasty Gal up with a proper website, she also decided to launch her own. When her site went live it looked really wonderful . . . because it looked exactly like mine. The design was exactly like mine, the wording was exactly like mine. Everything was exactly like mine. I'd known she was launching a website, but assumed she had enough class to do something different. I had one phone call with her in which I told her to get some ideas of her own, and we never spoke again.

After this happened, I was obsessed with this incident. I talked about it all the time while rolling my eyes and thinking about how much she sucked. Finally, I did this so much that Gary pointed out I was obsessing about her so much that I was going to make her successful. I took this advice seriously, and decided then that I don't want to spend time thinking about things that I don't want to have a place in my life. You have to kick people out of your head as forcefully as you'd kick someone out of your house if you didn't want them to be there.

Naturally, every boyfriend comes with an ex-girlfriend, every business comes with competitors, but it is entirely up to you to decide how much time you spend thinking about them. Frankly, even if that girl your boyfriend used to make out with suddenly gets hit by a car (like you're secretly hoping she will), who cares? You're still you. The same goes for business: There's no karmic law that dictates your business will succeed if others fail, so why not just wish them well and get on with it?

Focus on the positive things in your life and you'll be shocked at how many more positive things start happening. But before you start to think you just got lucky, remember that it's magic, and you made it yourself.

7

I Am the Antifashion

Why fit in when you were born to stand out?

—*Dr. Seuss*

As the French philosopher Jean-Paul Sartre so poignantly put it, "Hell is other people." While I no longer agree with this sentiment, I can empathize with the guy. When I was about four or five, my parents threw me a birthday party. There was cake, presents, and a piñata. When the time came, I lined up, got blindfolded, spun around in circles, and whacked the poor papier-mâché donkey with a broomstick, just like all the other kids. Hitting something with a stick was very gratifying, but I had never seen a piñata before, and had no idea that there was any sort of end goal. Therefore, it came as a complete shock to me when another child's final whack knocked the donkey's head off; it split open, spilling its candy guts onto the ground. The sight of Tootsie Rolls and Starbursts turned the other kids into screaming primates and as they immediately dove for the candy, I stood frozen. I was completely unaware that such a treasure trove even existed inside that piñata, so instead of jumping into the melee to fight for my rights, I turned, ran straight to the nearest table, and promptly crawled under it. And there I stayed until the last sugar-sodden five-year-old party guest had left and I felt it was safe to emerge from my cave.

Twenty-five years later, I'm still not a huge fan of surprises.

This is your brain on introversion.

Though it might not seem like it from the outside, I'm actually an introvert. Common knowledge used to dictate that extroverts were outgoing and introverts were shy, and this certainly never applied to me. I'm about as far away as you can get from a shrinking violet. However, research over the last few years has been focused on how the two personality types are actually more defined by what energizes them. Extroverts get their energy from being around a lot of people, but introverts find large groups draining and require time alone to recharge.

Introverts and extroverts also process external stimuli via different pathways in the brain, which means that something an extrovert would find completely fun and novel—such as a bunch of kindergarteners rioting for candy—would be totally overwhelming to an introvert like me.

However, as a kid you're not self-aware enough to understand why you're different; you just know that you are. Being an only child meant that I naturally spent a ton of time alone. I preferred it this way and was never lonely. Yet at school this tendency to be alone made me feel weird. It was considered strange to want to be alone on the swings while everyone else was on the jungle gym, even if alone on the swings was where I was happiest. As a result I spent way too much time thinking about what other people thought about me, and what I could possibly do to make them like me more. Did they think my family's house was big enough? Did they think I was pretty? Did they like my backpack? I think it's cool, but what if this backpack makes me look like I'm in sixth grade when really I'm in seventh? Just typing that paragraph makes me exhausted, so I think it was no wonder that by the time I was a teenager, I ended up preferring to make tuna sandwiches at Subway, where at least I could be alone in my head, rather than subjecting myself to the nonstop emotional roller coaster they call adolescence.

Introverts are naturally more sensitive because they don't need a ton of dopamine, the "feel-good" neurotransmitter that your brain produces in response to positive stimuli. Conversely, extroverts can't get enough. They even love adrenaline, the chemical that your brain produces in the face of fear, so they need bigger and riskier situations to produce the same natural high that an introvert gets from just having a conversation with a close friend. Introverts are also more apt to pay attention to the small details (and an eBay store is a treasure trove of small details).

Much of the world, from school to the workplace, is set up to reward extroverts, and therefore it can be easier for introverts to feel overlooked or as if they don't measure up. For instance, even if you know all the answers but don't want to call attention to yourself by raising your hand, you might end up feeling, or being perceived as, less smart than the kids flailing their arms to get the teacher's attention. Same goes for work. Just remember, as Susan Cain writes in *Quiet*, "There's zero correlation between being the best talker and having the best ideas."

In business, a disproportionate amount of importance is placed on the ability to network. If you don't thrive on going out and meeting a million people, you might end up feeling that you have less of a chance of getting ahead in your career. Also, introverts might hang back in meetings and thus not be perceived as "leadership material," even though introverted people frequently make more empathetic managers. As I've said before, part of the reason that I started Nasty Gal was that I wanted a job where I could be by myself and not have to deal with people. I wasn't great at in-person customer service, because I can't fake a smile to save my life, but it turned out that I was really good at it electronically. Over e-mail, eBay, and MySpace, I was a customer service queen—able to respond to people politely and genuinely, infusing everything with a digital smile. Psychologists now believe that social media is a really valuable tool for introverts, because it allows them to communicate and even network on their own terms.

Even though introverts might keep quiet during meetings, they have several tendencies that actually come in handy in the world of business: They make fewer risky financial decisions (hello, $1 million in the bank at Nasty Gal!), are more persistent when faced with a problem that isn't easily solvable, and can also be very creative. A lot of the world's great artists, thinkers, and even businesspeople are and were introverts (Albert Einstein, Bill Gates, and J. K. Rowling, to name a few), so in no way does being an introvert doom you into a life in the shadows.

Getting Off at the Wrong Stop

I think I got off on the wrong planet. Beam me up, Scotty, there's no rational life here.

—Robert Anton Wilson

I was once (and still am) a not-so-secret metalhead. I'll admit that sometimes feeling bad feels *good*. A lot of people poopoo downer music, but they must just be really well adjusted. Nothing, for me, feels more comforting than the sound of an angry, misunderstood man.

There is a great song, "Born Too Late," by a band called Saint Vitus that I have always loved. I can still recite some of the lyrics by heart, because they're just too good. And by good, naturally, I mean *bad*.

Every time I'm on the street
People laugh and point at me
They laugh about my length of hair
And the out-of-date clothes I wear
They say my songs are much too slow
But they don't know the things I know.

I have a friend who told me something recently that really resonated. He said that he felt like he'd "gotten off at the wrong stop," as if there's a bus traveling through space and time that randomly opens its doors and drops souls off to live through whatever time they're assigned. I don't believe we're all fit for the time we're assigned. It's a weird world we live in, and until time travel exists we've all got to make the most of where we land.

Failure Is Your Invention

Life isn't about finding yourself. Life is about creating yourself.

—*George Bernard Shaw*

I gave up a long time ago on finding anything that was 100 percent, totally "me." I was not only open to trying on different lifestyles, I forced such experimentation upon myself—always knowing that I'd evolve past it, rarely surprised when I was ready to move on and never so attached that it hindered my growth.

Strangely, I think this attitude paid off when I started the business. From Nasty Gal's inception, I have always viewed the business as a work in progress. I constantly tweak and move on, peeling back layers of the onion as new ones arrive. If something didn't work—like if I put a dress up for auction and no one was bidding on it—I didn't just assume that no one wanted it. I just tried something else. I rewrote the product description, or swapped out the thumbnail because I thought that maybe people couldn't judge the silhouette correctly from the original picture I'd posted. I never assumed that I'd just done my best job the first time around.

Your challenge as a #GIRLBOSS is to dive headfirst into things without being too attached to the results. When your goal is to gain experience, perspective, and knowledge, failure is no longer a possibility. Failure is *your* invention. I believe that there is a silver lining in everything, and once you begin to see it, you'll need sunglasses to combat the glare. It is she who listens to the rest of the world who fails, and it is she who has enough confidence to define success and failure for herself who succeeds. These words were not invented for an incremental life. "Success" and "failure" serve a world that is black-and-white. And as I said before, it's all just kinda gray. This may sound sad, or boring, but it's actually quite empowering. It's not the prescription that many books may suggest exists, but it allows you to self-prescribe. And to self-subscribe.

You Belong Wherever You Want to Belong

Be yourself; everyone else is already taken.

—*Oscar Wilde*

There's a certain freedom to being an outsider. You do what you want, say what you want, and move on when you've worn out your welcome. In the past seven years, I've gone from being a nobody with no job and no insurance to someone who is seen as a leader and a role model. I was once told by a big-shot CEO that if I'm in an elevator with employees and chat with one but not the others, it signifies to everyone that the person I spoke to is more important than the others. To put it plainly, I exist under a microscope.

It's been rough getting used to the fact that what I say matters, whether it is good or bad, and holy shit, people actually want to talk to me. When we have our all-hands meetings, I am required to stand in front of two hundred people and talk about everything that's happening within the business while simultaneously seeming like I didn't have a bad morning and also possess every answer to the company's problems. I've asked myself, *Who am I to hold all of these other people captive while I blather and make bad jokes?* Oh shit, I'm the boss, that's who. Some people become CEOs for this exact reason—because they like to be in the spotlight—but it doesn't come naturally to me, and I don't know that it ever will. I no longer expect anyone to throw a rotten tomato at me and yell, "Off the stage, freak!" but the whole thing is still pretty surreal.

I've played with a lot of different lifestyles and identities. When I was living in Olympia, I snuck into a high school prom and danced with the cutest underclassmen I could find. I dressed up like a soccer mom to steal a loaf of bread. Never in my life, though, did I ever imagine that the role that I would actually end up inhabiting was that of a CEO. I felt like a fraud for a long time, as if there were no way in hell I was qualified. *Who gave this freak the keys?* I thought to myself, wondering if, and when, I'd ever be found out. I refused to think of people I met through business as friends. My real friends were weirdos from San Francisco who were broke, loved obscure elf metal, and celebrated 6/6/06 with me like it was Christmas. I kept telling myself that Danny, my investor, wasn't my friend, even though we had great conversations over dinner and I loved his wife. I thought that people like Danny couldn't be my real friends, because they were from this pedigreed world of MBAs and real careers, whereas I was just an interloper in a Black Sabbath T-shirt.

Finally, though, I arrived at a point where I decided this was bullshit. I stopped feeling as if I didn't belong anywhere, and realized that I belonged anywhere I wanted to be— whether that was a boardroom, business class, or on stage at a *Women's Wear Daily* CEO Summit. Today, I consider Danny my peer. Sometimes I can even get him to laugh at a fart joke.

Nasty Gal has been my MBA. I've learned to not be shy about stopping someone in the middle of a presentation to ask him to please clarify something because I don't know what he's talking about. If I still don't get it, I'll tell him so and ask him to explain it again. Sometimes I can practically hear the eyes rolling around the room—but given that I'm making decisions that involve so much money and so many people, I can't afford to pretend to know what's up. When you run a company the size of mine, you're not the only one who ends up paying for your mistakes. I could act like a CEO or I could really *be* a CEO, which means doing whatever I need to do (including asking obvious questions) to make the best decision for my company. No matter where you are in life, you'll save a lot of time by not worrying too much about what other people think about you. The earlier in your life that you can learn that, the easier the rest of it will be. You is who you is, so get used to it.

On Being a Freak

I like being myself. Myself and nasty.

—Aldous Huxley

When you accept yourself, it's surprising how much other people will accept you, too. As a company, Nasty Gal sits half in the fashion world and half in its own galaxy. I've never felt that more acutely than when I go to New York Fashion Week. I absolutely hate Fashion Week. It hurts me from the inside out. Let me break down Fashion Week for you, and I apologize if I am shattering your dreams of glamour and sophistication.

You are assigned a piece of bench in a too-hot or too-cold warehouse that is hard to get to because all the cabs are taken and the subway is not a choice due to your absurd-ass shoes. The piece of bench assigned to you is not even as wide as your butt, and someone is probably sitting on it. You are forced to either act like an asshole and confront that someone and tell him or her to move, or you go and put your butt down in someone else's assigned piece of bench, at which point that person will be forced to act like an asshole and come along and tell you to move. At this point, you couldn't care less about the clothes that you're about to see; you wish you were back in your hotel room eating glutinous pancakes and wearing sweats.

I'm not a blogger, I'm not an editor, and my company doesn't buy luxury brands, so even though I've been written about on Style.com and in such magazines as *Elle*, whenever I go to a fashion party I feel like Lindsay Lohan in *Mean Girls*, when she shows up to the Halloween party in a nightgown and buck teeth while everyone else is wearing lingerie and bunny ears. All of a sudden I revert to being an insecure thirteen-year-old, wondering if I'm wearing the right brand of shoes, and are they the right season? If so, are they the right color? Barf. It's a high school outfit contest, and I'd rather be working.

Nasty Gal is antifashion in that we encourage girls to choose what fashion means to them. We aren't just following, and neither are our customers. I'm getting more and more comfortable with one foot in the fashion world and one foot out. As I've gotten to know more people in the fashion industry, it's been refreshing to realize that a lot of them respect me because, as an outsider, I have a unique point of view.

Had I tried to fit in, Nasty Gal would have crashed and burned a long time ago. The last thing the world needs is another boring person or another boring brand, so embrace all the things that make you different. Alter your clothes all you want, but don't you *dare* alter your inner freak—she's got your back as much as I do.

Getting What You Want Even When You No Longer Want It

Far and away, the hardest thing for me to get used to about Nasty Gal's meteoric rise is that my own profile has risen with it. For years I prided myself on being anonymous, an expert at the art of avoiding human interaction. But today I could be walking along picking my nose, grabbing my boyfriend's butt, or trying on lip gloss in Sephora when suddenly someone sidles up to me and says, "You know, I really love Nasty Gal."

There's no way around it: The success of Nasty Gal means that my life has permanently changed. I've been tagged on Twitter by people who saw me going through airport security, running down a mountain in Big Sur, and sitting in the driveway of my own house. I've had people I don't know come up to me at parties and introduce themselves by saying, "Hey, I heard we're neighbors!" They're thrilled, but I'm thinking, *Who are you and how do you know where I live?*

I once Instagrammed a picture of my poodle, Donna, without realizing that my phone number was visible on her tag. When I started to get calls and texts from strangers, I was forced into changing the number that I'd had for years.

Once, at a meeting with my bank, they gave me a gift. It was a book called *Silent Safety: Best Practices for Protecting the Affluent*. The book had chapters with titles such as "Yacht Security" and "Surviving a Hostage Situation." I thought it was absurd, until it began to terrify me. Holy shit, is this the way I'm supposed to live my life now?

I'm not complaining—this is all just stuff that I'm still getting used to. For example, it's weird to go through life being congratulated on a daily basis. In a single year, I had a profile in *Forbes*, was on the cover of *Entrepreneur*, listed on

CNNMoney's 40 Under 40, Inc.com's 30 Under 30, and named by *Inc.* magazine as the fastest-growing retailer in the country. Our office has consumed a whole hell of a lot of champagne, but how many bottles can you pop? Remember, #GIRLBOSS: It's not cool to get drunk on your own success.

PORTRAIT OF A #GIRLBOSS:

Norma Kamali, Fashion Designer and Entrepreneur

When I was young, I was so smart and was sure I could do anything. I was convinced I could be a painter and did everything from intensive life drawing while worshipping Michelangelo to studying art history and painting with a passion. My mother convinced me that painting may not be the best way to earn a living and pay rent.

I was very lucky to receive scholarships and grants for my paintings, but also a scholarship to FIT. There I studied fashion illustration and found my way into design after traveling to London in the 1960s. I opened a store in 1967 and have been in business ever since.

I learned early on the motto "Know thyself." I think if you have a unique point of view and stay relevant and authentic, you will make an impression. You have to be excited and passionate about your ideas to make them work. Chances are it will take twenty of those good ideas before one sticks and has a chance to become real, but a good idea is only good if there is a well-thought-out plan to make it a reality.

The most important thing to do is to take risks. The risks are where breakthroughs happen, and big shifts take you to new places and create opportunities. They can be really scary and intimidating, but that means it is taking you out of your comfort zone.

All designers look at life through a creative lens and are inclined to create their brand of beauty in their everyday lives. I am happy to say it brings me joy and I love doing it for others as well. I prefer to be creative first and famous last.

My mother told me when I was eleven years old, "Learn how to take care of yourself so that the man you marry is the man you choose to be with and not just the man who will take care of you." Women have an opportunity now to change the world. We are all aware of the movement toward women becoming a significant force in the chance for real dynamic change. When things aren't working so well, like now, it becomes a disruptive time.

My advice would be to dream and never stop dreaming. Making my dreams come true has always inspired me to work hard. One dream is never enough, and your dream can be molded and finessed along the way to become relevant and successful.

8

On Hiring, Staying Employed, and Firing

I never dreamed about success.
I worked for it.

—*Estée Lauder*

It's a huge testament to Nasty Gal that so many people want to work there. I'm incredibly proud of the team that I've hired. You would be hard-pressed to find a harder-working, more creative bunch of freaks anywhere in the world.

In my relatively short career, I've hired and been hired multiple times, fired and been fired a few times, and stayed employed once (yay, Nasty Gal!). That qualifies me to give advice on all three.

On Hiring

I was always able to get a job—although keeping it was sometimes a different story. Even when I applied for a minimum wage job at the outlet mall, I handed in a résumé with my application, and that résumé always had an objective neatly typed out at the top, such as "To procure a sales position at a respected retail establishment." If I dropped an application off and wasn't able to speak with the manager in person, I always followed up with a phone call, or dropped by again to annoy the establishment into remembering me. I hit the manager with everything that I had, convincing him or her that I wanted nothing more in the world than a chance to spend my afternoons helping old ladies slide their feet into a pair of orthopedic pumps.

And that's my first rule of hiring: Although playing hard to get might be cute in the dating world, it won't fly with potential employers. They don't have time to court you, so you had better romance the hell out of them. Competition is stiff—particularly in a tight job market and tough economy—so unless you can sweep someone off his or her feet, unemployed you will stay. Ideally, you'll be applying for a job that you genuinely think is interesting and exciting. If you're not, #GIRLBOSS, then fake it till you make it.

The Necessary Evil: Cover Letters

It had long since come to my attention that people of accomplishment rarely sat back and let things happen to them. They went out and happened to things.

—*Leonardo da Vinci*

I love cover letters. Yes, they're painful to write—and trust me, often painful to read—but a cover letter is your first opportunity to make an impression on your future boss. As an employer, when I go through hundreds of applications from people who all have very similar-sounding education and experience, cover letters are the only glimpse I have into a person's personality. Cover letters separate the #GIRLBOSSes from the girls. That said, few people seem to know how to make a cover letter sing. It's incredible how low the bar is, so you're in luck! I'm about to help you navigate the weird, unnatural world of putting your best foot forward in a few paragraphs.

Cover Letter Mistake #1: The cover letter is all about what you want. Nasty Gal gets so many cover letters that detail a "passion for fashion" and then proceed to talk about how this job will help the applicant pursue her interests, gain more experience, and explore new avenues.

If a cover letter starts out like this, I usually end up reading the first couple of sentences before hitting the delete button. Why? Because I don't care about what a job will do for you and your personal development. I know that sounds harsh, but I don't know you, so the fact that you want to work for my company does not automatically mean that I have an interest in helping you grow your career. I have a business that is growing by the day, so I want to know what *you* can do for *me*. It's as simple as that.

Cover Letter Mistake #2: Your cover letter basically says that nothing you've ever done is even remotely applicable to the job you're applying for. When we posted a job for a copywriter a while back, I remember reading an application from someone who had graduated with an MFA in fiction from the Iowa Writers' Workshop, one of the most prestigious writing programs in the country. This is what stood out the most to me about her résumé, but it wasn't even mentioned in her cover letter. A cover letter can connect the dots between where you've been, where you are, and where you're trying to go.

Unless you spell out what that is in your cover letter, your potential employer may never know. If you're light on extracurricular activities coming out of college because you had to work forty hours a week to pay for it, then by all means make sure that it's obvious. Someone who shows evidence of financial responsibility and work ethic can be just as impressive, if not more so, than someone who was president of the Bowling Society or secretary of the Wine Tasting Club. Even if you're applying to work at a bowling alley that serves only wine. (Okay, maybe not then.)

Cover Letter Mistake #3: You give so-called constructive criticism—without being asked. When I'm interviewing people, I'll often ask what they think Nasty Gal could be doing better, and I am genuinely interested to hear what they have to say. But detailing the ways that you think a company needs to improve in a cover letter is like meeting someone for the first time and telling her that you think she'd be so much cuter if she lost just five pounds. It's distasteful. You would be surprised to learn how often people think that dedicating their entire cover letter to detailing Nasty Gal's flaws is a good idea. It's not. I always want to write these people back and say, "Opinions are like assholes; everybody's got one." But I don't, because I'm a #GIRLBOSS so I keep it professional-ish.

Cover Letter Mistake #4: Either you didn't take the time to read it, or you just really, really can't write. In Jason Fried's book *Rework*, he writes that one of the smartest investments a business can make is in hiring great writers, and I completely agree. No matter what you are hired to do, you will be infinitely better off if you are able to clearly communicate your ideas. We can't all be Shakespeare, but spend some time on your cover letter and have someone else look it over to make sure it reads well. If it looks like you don't care about your cover letter and rushed through it, then I'm going to assume that you will be just as careless in your work.

On that note, another piece of advice: Spell-check exists for a reason; use it, but don't rely on it. If you don't know the difference between "there," "their," and "they're," you're in bad shape. We're lucky enough in the United States to get by with only having to know *one* language, so nail the one we've got! If I have to read another e-mail that begins with "I've followed Naty Gal since the eBay days," I will throw myself out the window. As we are only on the third floor, that means that I will have to deal with a really gnarly sprained ankle and it will be all your nonthinking, non-spell-checking fault.

The Résumé: More Than Just a Bunch of Mumbo Jumbo

There is no question that putting together a résumé sucks. How can one boil down all of one's skills, experience, intellect, and advantages onto one piece of paper? I know it's weird, but it's a currency we all have to accept. Regardless of how lame you think the concept of a résumé is, you should still make sure that yours is as far away from lame as you can possibly get. As a visual person, I love a creative résumé. I'm not a fan of templates—putting a little effort in on the design side will show that you care as much as I do about things looking good.

I like real words on a résumé—that means I want to read it and understand it. If you had a job as a marketing manager, be very didactic when you're listing what you did. "Built brand relationships within the creative community"—really, what does that *mean*? "Curated artwork, booked bands, secured beverage sponsors, and oversaw budget for an ongoing series of monthly art exhibits"—now, *that* makes sense, and also tells me that you're able to navigate the practicalities that are necessary to bring your ideas to life. We don't need people who just *have* ideas; we need people who can also *execute* them. If you've made some shit happen, make sure your résumé reflects that—this is one of the few places where it's actually good to brag a bit.

The Interview: Don't Blow It

You wrote a cover letter that was so good it made my mascara run, and now you have an interview. Have you ever walked into a party and felt like everyone was staring at you in judgment? This is why you should not smoke weed at parties. But in all seriousness, at a job interview, this is exactly what happens. Job interviews are intense, and unfortunately, there's no one-size-fits-all study guide for breezing through them. You can say all the right things, have all the right experience, and still not be the right fit for a job. There are millions of other unpredictable behind-the-scenes reasons a job does or does not work out.

When someone's right for a role, sometimes both parties just know. After a long and grueling search for a marketing position, I finally met someone who I clicked with right away. We had lunch on Thursday, brunch on Sunday, and on Monday he came by the office and left with an offer letter in his hand. He is a little bit wacko (and so am I) and though professional, there wasn't much pretense. I liked that he understood Nasty Gal, was excited about the brand, and was an abstract thinker. His ideas weren't just like everyone else's. When I made him an offer, he said, "You're out of your mind!" He meant it as a compliment, and I took it as such.

A #GIRLBOSS knows that she may not nail it on the first try, and that's okay. Remember to be open and keep your head up when something doesn't work out. However, even the best of us can suffer sweaty armpits and a dry mouth during an interview. Here are a few things to know that will hopefully make it easier.

Networking Is Not Just for Creeps

LinkedIn has made it easier than ever before to connect with people who can help you get ahead. Whether they are doing what you want to be doing, or working where you want to be working, it can be as simple as a "Hey! I came across your profile and would love to grab a coffee sometime. Your experience is really interesting." You can go into a little detail about why you think they're interesting, or what you're working on, but some flattery never hurts. As an admitted "beast" on LinkedIn, I know this from experience. I've hired C-level executives on LinkedIn, creatives on Facebook, and even an intern on Instagram. Treat your LinkedIn profile like an online résumé. Please do not wear sunglasses in your profile photo or self-identify as "visionary." No profile at all is better than a half-completed one that you stopped caring about after getting thirteen connections. Again, a LinkedIn profile can be a first impression, so if it looks like you don't pay much attention to detail, a recruiter can only assume that you'd take the same approach with your job.

I will tell you that networking is yet another subject where my mantra of "You don't get what you don't ask for" applies. I'm friends with Mickey Drexler, the CEO of J.Crew, not because we were introduced (though that would have been much cooler), but because I hunted him down, and hunted him down again. He's a great friend and mentor now, and all it took was a nice e-mail to get some of the best business advice I'll ever have.

Be Prepared to Get Real

I didn't always get the jobs that I applied for. When I applied at Nordstrom, I didn't get the job because they asked me real questions, such as What did I want out of my career? If you're going into a job interview, you should always be prepared to have smart answers to smart questions but also smart answers to dumb questions, and it doesn't hurt to practice. Someone will likely ask you, "What do you like to do in your free time?" and even if your hobbies include watching reruns of *Roseanne*, you should have a more appropriate answer prepared. The more interesting, memorable, and even unusual that answer is, the better, because as much as your potential employer wants you to be a total rock star at your job, she is also considering you as someone with whom she is going to end up spending eight hours a day.

One of the most standard interview questions is "What do you think is your biggest weakness?" It's a question that I ask often, and I want people to answer honestly. Do not answer this question by disguising one of your strengths as a weakness. When people answer me with "My biggest weakness is that I'm a perfectionist," or "I'm always early to meetings," I just groan (but only on the inside; I'm not that rude) and figure that these are people who aren't really being honest with themselves. I like honesty and I value curiosity, and people who are honest and curious aren't generally impeccable. A #GIRLBOSS knows where she excels and where she could use some work, so get to know yourself and your weaknesses. And as you can't predict every question you're going to be asked, become familiar with the role you are interviewing for and prepare. Research the company and the job itself, and spend some time thinking about what you, personally, can bring to the table. Also, be up-front about what you want. Employment is a two-way agreement, so let's be adults. If you are looking for a job that doesn't include certain factors, speak up. The last thing you want is to show up on day one and find out that the job you thought you wanted was in fact the total opposite.

But Not Too Real

I've interviewed so many people by now that I swear I can smell crazy a mile away. If you go into too much detail about how you parted with your previous employer, it's a red flag. Even if your boss was a raging lunatic, or you found yourself in a position where you had to work twenty-hour days, if you launch into this in an interview, you will come across as an entitled complainer—and an indiscreet one, to boot. I recently interviewed someone who described why she had left her previous two jobs: She left one because she got tired of going to the same place every day, and she left the other one because she asked for an assistant and her boss said no. Hello? If we hire you, you're going to have to come here every day, and you basically just explained that you bail whenever you don't get what you want.

Also, even though our office is a pretty casual environment, don't interpret this as a free pass to be informal. One of our employees recently interviewed someone, and the first thing the candidate said to her when she walked in the room was, "Oh, you look comfy." And . . . done. If you're nervous and don't know what to say, just say nothing. Making small talk about what someone is wearing is just another form of unsolicited feedback. Knowing when to speak up and when to shut up will get you very far not only in business, but in life.

It also always causes me to raise an eyebrow when someone says he or she has been a consultant for the past few years, but can't elaborate on that or put it into concrete accomplishments. It's a mistake to try to bluff about your experience because such posturing usually starts to crack after a few smart questions. But if you were legitimately freelancing, consulting, or running your own business for a while, that says a lot about you. As an entrepreneur, I have a ton of respect for anyone who's willing to give working for themselves a go. Even if you eventually decided it wasn't for you, this kind of experience can still make you stand out.

Interview No-No's That May Doom You to Unemployment

- Chewing gum
- Bringing things with you—a beverage, a pet, a boyfriend, a child
- Leaning back in your chair and crossing your arms
- Staring at the floor, out the window, or at the interviewer's boobs
- Picking your nose or your nails
- Having your phone even visible
- Having zero questions
- Asking so many questions that it seems like you're interviewing the interviewer
- Not writing a thank-you e-mail or note—I especially love a handwritten note because to me, someone who knows to have good manners knows how to get what she wants in this world
- Dressing like you're headed to a nightclub instead of a job interview

- As a female, thinking that you don't have to wear a bra, even if you're interviewing at a company with a name like Nasty Gal

So You Got a Job? Awesome! Now Keep It!

That's when I first learned that it wasn't enough to just do your job, you had to have an interest in it, even a passion for it.

—*Charles Bukowski*

Nasty Gal is not a traditional nine-to-five company. Everyone here is very passionate about Nasty Gal and believes in what we're doing. We work hard because we're a bunch of #GIRL-BOSSes (and some #DUDEBOSSes) and we know that we're working on something that's bigger than just us. If you're looking for a job where you can show up, make no impact on the world, and watch a lot of cat videos, this is not the place for you. However, I do know an art school lobby in San Francisco that might be hiring. . . .

As a #GIRLBOSS is ambitious by nature, I'm going to assume that once you get a job, you want to do it well and eventually move up. And though every company is different, here are a few pointers on how to make that happen.

The Four Words Thou Shalt Never Mutter

You want to know what four words I probably hate the most? "That's not my job." Nasty Gal is not a place where these four words fly. At the end of the day, we're all here for one reason and one reason only—to make the company succeed—and there will undoubtedly be a day (perhaps every day) when you will have to roll up your sleeves and dive in where you're needed. When a company is growing quickly, there will be times when there are holes—there is a job that needs to be done, and there is no one there to do it.

A few years back, our warehouse manager gave his two weeks' notice exactly two weeks before Black Friday. On Thanksgiving night, our creative director, merchandisers, girls from the buying team, me, and whomever else we were able to round up headed down there and shuffled around a dusty warehouse until 4:00 A.M., scanning and reclassifying all of our inventory so we could ensure that the people who shopped with us on one of the most important retail days of the year actually got the clothes that they ordered. At 2:00 A.M., as I was counting and recounting bustiers, I did not give a shit whether people were creative or whether they loved fashion— I was just thankful to have employees who were willing, even enthusiastic, to step up and work hard.

In an ideal world you'd never have to do things that are below your position, but this isn't an ideal world and it's never going to be. You have to understand that even a creative job isn't just about being creative, but about doing the work that needs to get done. The #GIRLBOSS who is willing to do a job that is below her—and above—is the one who stands out. Above, you ask? Yes. Sometimes you'll find an opportunity to step in when your boss is out, or just swamped, and show your worth. You're as smart as she is, anyway, so figure it out as you go and make it look like child's play. It's that attitude, and behavior, that will get you ahead.

God—and a Promotion—Is in the Details

Be a nice person at work. It doesn't matter how talented you are; if you are a total terror to work with, no one will want to keep you around. And the worst kind of mean is selective mean—people who are nice to their boss and superiors, but completely rude to their peers or subordinates. If you are a habitual bitch to the front desk girl, the security guard, or even the Starbucks staff downstairs, that news will eventually make its way up the chain, and the top of the chain ain't gonna like it.

Own up to your mistakes and apologize for them. Everyone will make a mistake at some point, and the sooner you can admit where you went wrong, the sooner you can start to fix it. Be honest with yourself about yourself and your abilities. Many people accept titles that are beyond their experience to only later find themselves up to their neck in problems they can't solve, and too embarrassed to admit they weren't qualified in the first place. And what's the first rule about holes? If you're in one, stop digging.

Boundaries, Found

Your boss is not your friend and if you're the boss, your employees aren't your friends. I learned this the hard way when I was out to dinner one night with someone who used to report to me. It was right after I bought the Porsche, and I was babbling on about how flashy it was, and how much of a cheese ball I sometimes felt like driving it. However, instead of listening as a friend, she took this honesty about my insecurities as an opportunity to insult, and said, "Well, you know, you'd better be careful, because people are saying 'Oh, now I'm doing my job to pay for a Porsche.'" While I still don't believe anyone but the person I was with had an issue with my auto purchase, it quickly had me bawling into my rosé. Yet it taught me a lesson: While it's okay to be friends with my investor, it's not okay to be friends with my direct reports. If you need someone to listen as you drag your psyche across the coals, find a friend or a therapist, but don't do it with someone you're expected to manage on a daily basis.

At a company like Nasty Gal, which seems very informal and where there are a lot of young people, the managerial lines can sometimes get blurry. If you treat your reports like your peers, your team won't respect you further down the road when you have to play a trump card or put your foot down. I'll go for drinks with people, I'll dance at parties, but at the end of the day people know that when I give someone a deadline, it's not up for discussion.

You Are Not a Special Snowflake

Millennials got so many participation trophies growing up that a recent study showed that 40% believe
they should be promoted every two years, regardless
of performance.

—*Joel Stein in* Time *magazine*

From one speed demon to another, let me be straight with
you: Slow your roll. You got a job, that's great, but you need
to get your hands dirty and spend time proving yourself before you ask for a raise or a promotion. Four months are not
enough, and neither are eight. At the bare minimum, you
need to be in your position for a year before you ask for a
raise or title change. Even then, that's if and only if you've
been going above and beyond, doing work that's outside
your job description, and generally making yourself completely indispensable to your employer.

A lot of people in my generation don't seem to get
that you have to work your way up. An entry level job is
precisely that—entry level—which means that you're not
going to be running the show or getting to work on the most
fun and creative projects. I've heard so many people in their
twenties complain about their jobs because they "have so
much more to offer," but first and foremost, you have to do
the job that you're there to do. I don't care if filing invoices is

beneath you. If you don't do it, who do you think is going to? Your boss? Nope. That's why she hired *you*.

I know you've probably grown up with your parents telling you that you're special every day for the past twenty years—it's okay, my parents did too—but you still have to show up and work hard just like everybody else. If you're a #GIRLBOSS, you should want to work harder than everybody else.

It takes a lot more than just knowing how to put an outfit together to succeed in the fashion industry, so more power to you if this is where you want to be; just don't expect it to be an extended trip to the mall. And if you're a cute girl expecting to just get by on her looks, go apply elsewhere. We've already got a ton of cute girls working at Nasty Gal, and they're all busting ass.

The Firing Line

There is no way around it, and it doesn't matter which side of the desk you're on: Getting fired straight-up sucks. One of the many jobs I was fired from was a sales associate job at a luxury shoe store in San Francisco. I was a crummy twenty-one-year-old—not as dirty as I had been, but still not completely clean—hawking shoes by Maison Martin Margiela, Miu Miu, and Dries van Noten with quadruple-digit price tags. At that time I stayed out all night and showed up to work semi-showered, wearing the same red polyester flares day after day as I sold

Prada pumps to rich ladies. I didn't care about Prada and I didn't get that I was supposed to pretend. As I write this, I am in love with a particular pair of Prada shoes that I am considering buying, so oh how times have changed, but back then I was indignant about it—"Who is spending *this* kind of money on shoes?"

I made $12 an hour with no commission as these women from Pacific Heights (a pretty chichi neighborhood in San Francisco) would come in and I would have to smile and be all like "*Hiiiiiiiiii*, how are *youuuuuu*? Let me know if there's anything I can help you *withhhh*," while inside I was thinking, *I hate you*. The store made the salespeople wear the shoes too, so I had a pair of Dries van Noten pumps that were so scuffed they could have been vintage. They weren't special to me, so I wore them to work and burrito shops alike. On Sundays I worked by myself, and was given thirty minutes to close the store for my lunch break. Time came, I flipped the sign on the door, locked up, and walked down the street to order a hamburger. The burger took forever and I was hungry. This, coupled with my pathetic sense of time, caused me to be super late to open the store back up. When you make $12 an hour and you're spending $8 on a burger, you had damn well better make it count.

When I finally made it back to the store well past my thirty-minute lunch break, the owner was there. I'd been perpetually late, perpetually grimy, and I'm sure that this had been a long time coming. She collected my key, gave me my final paycheck, and sent me on my way. This was actually the last time that I was fired. Seven years later, I can't quit and no one can fire me.

Telling Someone "You're Fired"

Generally I like other people to fire, because it's always a lousy task.

—*Donald Trump*

Sadly, it wasn't too long after I took Nasty Gal off eBay that I had to fire someone for the first time. When I first hired someone to oversee shipping, the business was still just Christina and me. We were twenty-two-year-olds managing a grown man who, on his third day of work, asked if he could leave early because it was "grocery day" for his family. Sweet, but no. It was also apparent that he had never used a computer before. He was completely stumped when a box popped up on the screen. "It says 'Norton AntiVirus.' What do I do?" Christina and I both screamed, "Oh my God, just click the 'X'!" I started to panic, because I had hired this guy to make my life easier and it was clear that this was not going to be the case at all.

We also hired a copywriter who, in my weaker moments, I started to think was a spy sent by a competitor to sabotage the business from the inside—because there was no way in hell his mistakes could be for real. Time after time, I would say, "Please use spell-check and stop having so many typos," but then everything he wrote looked like it had been done by my poodle who was pecking at the keyboard with her nose.

I knew he had to go, and it was tortuous for me. I read up on all the legal responsibilities of firing someone, and went through all the different scenarios in my head—if he said this, I was going to say that; if he asked that, I was going to explain it like this. When I finally, practically hyperventilating, sat him down and told him we were letting him go, he was totally calm about it. "Okay." He shrugged. "No problem." And he left.

The harsh truth is that not everyone you hire is going to work out. It's impossible to know everything about a person's talent, judgment, and character without actually working with him or her. In many cases, the people who don't work out are people about whom I had second thoughts from day one. However, sometimes it is simply a matter of a fast-growing company growing faster than the people inside it. The person who was right for the job a year ago might not be right for the job a year from now. Don't get me wrong: I'm loyal to every person I've hired. But my loyalty lies with the greater business, which means the hundreds of others whose jobs could be at stake if we have the wrong person in the wrong role. I know this sounds harsh, but it's that level of objectivity that leaders need to have. And leading is, after all, what I'm ultimately here to do.

If someone who is working for you keeps screwing up, make sure you talk to her about it. There's always the slight off chance that maybe that employee doesn't know that she is doing anything wrong and it's something that she can easily fix. Everyone should be given the opportunity to improve. But if you think you're going to have to fire someone, start documenting everything. People who get fired love to say shit like, "The only reason I got fired was because that bitch didn't like me." Chances are that if you're ready to fire someone, you probably don't like that person. And that's okay. Just keep your cool and be professional, because it's not about that. It's because someone sucks that you have to do this, not because you suck. If your company has a human resources department, make sure that they're aware of what's going on. If you can write someone up, write someone up.

Sadly, sometimes the ship can't be righted. So when it comes time to actually do it, don't pussyfoot about and don't act like a baby. As Voltaire said, "With great power comes great responsibility." If you want to be a boss and be treated like a boss, then firing someone is in your boss-size job description. Don't ever try to impress upon the person you're about to fire how hard the situation is for you, because that person is losing his or her job, so it's obviously harder on them. Resist the urge to overexplain or even to apologize. Keep it as short and sweet as you possibly can, because the more personal you try to make it, the more personally your soon-to-be ex-employee is going to take it. However, it doesn't hurt to take a few minutes to put yourself in their shoes, and consider how you would want to be treated if you were in that position. And if you both learn from your lessons, neither of you will make the mistakes that led to that situation again.

Hearing "You're Fired"

I didn't see it then, but it turned out that getting fired from Apple was the best thing that could have ever happened to me.

—*Steve Jobs*

Though I was fired a few times, and usually from jobs I couldn't have cared less about, I still was never like the copywriter who just shrugged and walked out the door. Getting fired was always a big deal to me. It's a bit like having someone break up with you. Even if you know it wasn't the right situation, and that you'll be way better in the long run, it's still rejection. And rejection sucks.

But getting fired, especially from a job you're not actually that into, isn't the end of the world. For me, getting fired from the shoe store was an opportunity to find a job with health insurance. And although I got the job at the art school primarily to fix my hernia, I ended up with a lot more than I bargained for: the inspiration to start something that led me to where I am today.

Getting fired can be a much-needed wake-up call, a push

in the right direction, or an escape route. Or it can just plain suck. But no matter what the details of the situation, how much you learn from it is entirely up to you. It can also be the end of the world (or at least feel like it) if you've got zero savings. If you're living paycheck to paycheck already, and all of a sudden there's no more paycheck, that's terrifying. I don't want to get all "told ya so," but the fact that you could get fired (and almost all of us could get fired) is all the more reason to consistently save 10 percent of those earnings. Instead of calling it a rainy-day fund, let's call it an oh-shit fund. And you'll be saying "oh shit" a whole lot less if you've got one.

Here is a list of things to *not* do if you get fired:

- Call anyone a bitch or an asshole, or any variations thereof
- Threaten to sue—if you do think you have a legitimate reason, talk to a lawyer before you do anything
- Try to get your former coworkers to take your side (as sympathetic as they might be, they're going to be worried about their own jobs)
- Take to the Internet to complain or talk shit about your boss or your former employer; people have a lot of Facebook friends these days, and chances are you have a couple on your friend list whom you've forgotten about
- Use the person who fired you as a reference without first asking him or her if it's cool

- Draw attention to yourself upon departure; flipping the bird to the executive team on your way out will not make things any better
- Have your mom or dad call (yep, this has happened)

Now, recently fired #GIRLBOSS, get thee on with thy life!

PORTRAIT OF A #GIRLBOSS:

Christene Barberich, Refinery29
Editor in Chief

I always knew I wanted to be a writer and an editor. There never was a choice, it's all I ever wanted to do. My first real publishing job was as an assistant at the New Yorker, *but my editorial training happened at* Gourmet *magazine. In terms of striking out on my own and being brave in my convictions, I learned that mostly by being freelance. I don't think you can truly know what you're made of until you are in charge of your days. How you use that time, and the work you pursue, teaches you so much about who you are and what you can become.*

It's possible I figured out what I wanted to do by people telling me I couldn't or shouldn't do it. It's really astounding how discouraging people can be, especially if it's something that seems particularly risky. But, you know, risk can be thrilling. I've often made hard career choices based on how scared I was of the opportunity. When the stakes are high—I'm talking cataclysmic-level change, success or failure—sometimes you just have to jump, screaming the whole fucking way. I don't know if there is any greater feeling than proving you are your own biggest advocate. And all that noise out there is seriously just bullshit.

My mom is the hardest worker I know. She taught me that showing up is the most important part of any role. And, of course, my team inspires me hourly! It is because of them that I read a lot and never, ever take anything for granted. Simply by being so smart and curious, they inspire me to be an excellent editor, a courageous leader, and someone who motivates them to create cool and special stuff. When you're collaborating with other people, it's important to know what you don't know and to find the best person in that area to teach you. Be a leader even in teams of one because in the beginning, there's a lot of that! You have to listen, really listen, and root for other people's success. That's a big one. Because it won't always be you, but eventually, it will be.

For me, creativity isn't just in my work—it's how I think and live my life. It's not necessarily about always creating something new, but simply having the space and freedom to let something special happen. It's how I bring beauty and joy into my surroundings and my relationships. I like to be challenged; seeing or *reading something that opens my eyes or gives me chills is the whole point of everything. My advice to aspiring #GIRLBOSSes: As hard as it is, stop caring so much about what other people think. Find a way to hear what you want. Recognize what is your dream. And then put everything you have into that: your work, the relationships you surround yourself with, the food you put in your body. Everything you have control over in your world should feed that dream and make you feel like a #GIRLBOSS!*

Taking Care of (Your) Business

*Things may come to those who wait,
but only the things left by those who hustle.*

—*Abraham Lincoln*

never started a business. I started an eBay store, and ended up with a business. I never would have done it had I known it was going to become this big. I was twenty-two and, like most twenty-two-year-olds, I was looking for a way to pay my rent and buy my Starbucks chai. Had someone shown me the future of where Nasty Gal would be in 2014, I would have gasped in revulsion, thinking, *Oh, hell no, that is way too much work.* The name of the company alone should clue you in to this fact—who would have thought that a company called Nasty Gal could be so successful? I sure as shit never intended to be saying those two words all day, every day, seven years later.

There are different kinds of entrepreneurs. There are the ones who start a business because they're educated and choose to, and the ones who do it because it is really the only option. I definitely fall into the latter category. I considered myself completely unemployable, and wanted to give one last shot at my ideal of being "jobless." And boy, did being jobless work for me.

Nasty Gal would have surely failed had it been my goal to grow a business to the size that I have today. When you begin with the finish line in mind, you miss all the fun stuff along the way. The better approach is to tweak and grow, tweak and grow. I call it the incremental potential. In e-commerce, you have to get everything right—from the marketing to the product descriptions to the checkout process. Because I started small, I think I inherently did that from the beginning. Customer service was my number one priority. A lot of people run their businesses like their customers are dummies. This is a mistake. If you're just out to take their money, they know it. But if you genuinely care about what you're doing, they will respond. I knew my customers and knew what they liked, because I was my customer. And rather than dictating what I thought my customers should buy and wear, I listened instead. If I bought something and they hated it, I moved on. Rather than force my idea of what Nasty Gal should be on my customers, I let them tell me along the way.

Nasty Gal felt like the best-dressed girl's best-kept secret—except that it was a secret she really wanted to share. As I mentioned earlier, one key to running a successful business is to know how to get free marketing. Rule number one? That's simple. Just do a good job. Through the styling, photography, and voice of the brand, Nasty Gal was an exciting place to shop, but if our customers weren't equally as stoked when they were holding one of our products in their hands, then that excitement lived and died on the Internet. I don't take it lightly when someone buys something from me. I know there are a million places where people can buy a dress, a crop top, or a pair of shoes, so I want to make sure that if someone is buying it from Nasty Gal, she feels like it's worth it. We're dressing girls for the best years of their lives, so whether you drop $300 or shop the sale section, I want you to look and feel like a million bucks.

Rule number two: Keep your promises. When girls

bought something from Nasty Gal, what they got in the mail was just as amazing as what they'd seen online. Customers became not only loyal, but also evangelical. They came back again and again, and shared their excitement with their friends—frequently on the Internet. It was the kind of natural word of mouth that can't be bought.

Rule number three: Give your customers something to share. Social media is built on sharing, and Nasty Gal was giving girls something amazing to share each and every day. Whether it was a crazy vintage piece, a quote, or a behind-the-scenes photo, we have always worked hard to create the best and most compelling images, words, and content for our customers.

At most companies the person manning the Twitter and Facebook accounts is far from the top of the food chain. But at Nasty Gal, even though I'm not always composing every tweet, I still read every comment. If our customers are unhappy about something, I hear it first. At other businesses, it might take months for customer feedback to filter up to the CEO, if at all. Social media allows me to have my ear to the ground even when I'm out pounding the pavement. When Nasty Gal joined Snapchat, it meant that I joined Snapchat. I sent out a few Snaps, and our customers responded in force. There's nothing more thrilling than sending private texts directly to a customer and seeing what she has to say in response.

Call me crazy, but I truly believe that Nasty Gal is a feeling. And though our community lives in many different places, it's that feeling that unifies our customers and makes us about much more than selling clothes.

The Incremental Potential

Author Malcolm Gladwell believes that one can be an expert at something after putting in ten thousand hours of practice. Needless to say, my ten thousand hours are far behind me. Had I waited to finish a business plan, or waited for investors to validate my idea, my ten-thousand-hour clock might never have begun. Don't get me wrong: I'm not knocking business plans. What I intend to illustrate is that *just going for it* can be much more rewarding. Business plans are just a starting point—the best entrepreneurs know to listen along the way and adjust things, including their business plan. This advice applies to life as well, dear #GIRLBOSS. Turn on the jets and ready, set, . . . listen.

Starting a business is risky no matter which way you look at it, but it's much riskier when you have a ton of overhead and money guys anxiously waiting to earn a return on their investment. Starting a business also takes a lot of personal sacrifice. If you start a business, expect that you're probably going to be broke for a long time. If you're not broke, consider yourself broke, because as we discussed earlier, it is shortsighted to pay yourself a big salary too early. Dream big all you want—that's what this entire book is about!—but know that the first step toward those dreams is probably going to be a small one.

Many people mistake the glamour of business for business. One of my pet peeves includes entrepreneurs who issue press releases about their new venture before making their first dollar. I waited until I knew for sure that I had something to say before talking to the press—about anything—which took about five years. While media coverage can boost sales and garner attention from the business community, tooting your own horn too early can put you under the spotlight when you're still figuring out the basics of running your business. I've seen many a start-up disappear after making a big splash in the press. Though I'm rarely surprised, it feels good to be the fabled turtle in this scenario rather than the hare.

I didn't know anybody to turn to for business advice, and because of this, people ask me all the time how I figured it out. Well, I figured it out by doing what I think is one of the best strategies for learning anything anywhere: I Googled it. There is a whole wide world of free education out there for anyone who wishes to take advantage of it. Granted, a book might cost you $13, but that's pennies compared with college tuition. When I needed to know what kinds of shelving to buy for the warehouse, I Google Image–searched "warehouse shelving" and spent an afternoon looking at pictures of shelves until I figured out which ones would be best for our needs.

I turned to YouTube to watch experts speak at conferences I wouldn't have been invited to even if I had been able to afford to attend. I learned a ton about how to structure Nasty Gal by looking at similar businesses to see who they had hired and were hiring. I then viewed those people's profiles on LinkedIn to see what type of experience it takes to do that job successfully. And while I took it all with a grain of salt, it got me far.

Nasty Gal is now big enough for me to be able to hire people who are experts in their respective fields. But don't be fooled: I'm still calling the shots. I hate it when I'm in a meeting with one of our top officers and someone addresses her the entire time, assuming that the "adult" in the room must be the one making the decisions. Don't you dare think that my shredded T-shirt makes me a sheep in wolf's clothing. I, like every #GIRLBOSS, am a wolf in wolf's clothing.

Entrepreneurialism Is an Eighteen-Letter Word

> All humans are entrepreneurs not because they should start companies but because the will to create is encoded in human DNA.
>
> —*Reid Hoffman, cofounder of LinkedIn*

I think everyone should tap into their entrepreneurial spirit. However, I don't think everyone should be an entrepreneur. Harvard Business School professor Howard Stevenson famously defined "entrepreneurship" as "the pursuit of opportunity without regard to resources currently controlled." I give a "hell yes" to that definition—you should take that spirit with you to whatever job you're doing or whatever project you're undertaking.

When I was twenty-two, the thought of rising up within an organization was completely incomprehensible. To me, office jobs were like school, where the best way to get along was to show up on time, not ask questions, follow all the rules, and not make a fuss. Again, not my jam. However, that accepted paradigm is changing, and faster than ever. As Seth Godin points out in his book *Linchpin*, our society's existing ideas of education and employment are held over from a time when most jobs were in factories. People were trained to do exactly what they were told, and only what they were told, in order to keep things running smoothly. Following the rules without question was precisely what got someone promoted. Thankfully, though, this is changing, and in *Linchpin*, Godin elaborates that "it's becoming clear that people who reject the worst of the current system are actually more likely to succeed." If you need proof of that, well, hi. Here I am.

What I'm getting at here is that you can be entrepreneurial without being an entrepreneur. Entrepreneurial people are passionate about what they do, comfortable with taking risks, and quick at moving on from failures. These are all things I look for in the people I hire. I want problem solvers who take nothing at face value. I want people who fight for their ideas, even fight with me. I want people who are comfortable with disagreement. And I need people who sometimes, after all of that, hear the word "no" and get right back up to work even harder. There are a lot of companies changing the way they do things right now. It's a pretty exciting time to be in business, but only if you're surrounded by exciting people.

The Nasty Gal Philosophy

Businesses often forget about the culture, and ultimately, they suffer for it because you can't deliver good service from unhappy employees.

—*Tony Hsieh, Zappos CEO and author of* Delivering Happiness

At Nasty Gal, we have something we like to call "Our Philosophy." It's a set of directives that align us to stay focused on what really matters. We designed them really nice and pretty, and have them posted up around our offices as a little daily reminder of why we're all here. Even if you never land that coveted buying job in our headquarters, these ideas can be applied to any career path you choose:

Nasty Gal Obsessed: We keep the customer at the center of everything we do. Without customers, we have nothing.

Own It: Take the ball and run with it. We make smart decisions, put the business first, and do more with less.

People Are Important: Reach out, make friends, build trust.

No Assholes: We leave our egos at the door. We are respectful, collaborative, curious, and open-minded.

Learn On: What we're building has never been built before—the future is ours to write. We get excited about growth, take intelligent risks, and learn from our mistakes.

Have Fun and Keep It Weird.

On Investors

When I lived in San Francisco, my friends and I existed far outside the tech scene that made our rents so expensive. Broke as a joke, drinking Amstel Light and disco dancing in dive bars, we couldn't have been further removed. VC might as well have stood for Velveeta cheese, for all I knew. I just wondered who all of these people were, walking around in their hoodies with their white earbuds. Little did I know they were the reason some of my favorite burrito joints had become extinct.

When the time came for me to grow familiar with the concept of investors, it was still pretty intimidating. My first meeting with venture capitalists was scary: for one, I had never been in a boardroom. And it didn't take me long to realize we were speaking completely different languages. I felt like a little kid who had no place at the table. For about a year after that, whenever anyone reached out about investing in Nasty Gal, I just didn't respond.

Then I had to fire a really senior executive. And though it had no linear relationship to taking investment, it was a pretty gnarly experience that drove home the fact that if I was going to be a CEO (which I already was) and run a really big, fast-growing company (which I already was), I was going to have to do some stuff I didn't like. I grew some balls and finally decided to answer some of those calls. I headed up to Silicon Valley to meet with investors.

In San Francisco I picked up my friend Diego, a fellow entrepreneur and one of the smartest people I know. He'd already been through the process of raising venture capital, so we powwowed in the car as I picked his brain. It was my crash course and I needed it: I was in and out of six meetings that day, all with different firms.

This time around I knew that I had nothing to lose: Nasty Gal was kicking ass, profitable, and had money in the bank. Either way, we were going to be fine. While most entrepreneurs meet investors with a presentation on what they plan to do with their business, I, being my PowerPoint–challenged self, arrived empty-handed. It turned out that Nasty Gal's strongest selling point wasn't what we were going to do, but what we'd already done.

"We're going to do one hundred million dollars this year."

"No, I've never borrowed a dime."

"No, I didn't go to college."

"No, I don't have previous experience running a business."

I got pretty accustomed to saying all of those things, and as I knocked down meeting after meeting, something pretty shocking dawned on me: Holy shit, these people are impressed.

Sand Hill Road is the legendary venture capital hub in Menlo Park between Stanford University and Silicon Valley. The people who sit in those offices operate in a very different paradigm than I do, spending their days talking business models and IPOs in a way that I never will. It was strangely encouraging for me to come out of nowhere with instant respect from people I felt were an entirely different species. Some of them wanted to be friends and others tried to appeal to my edgy side (and FYI, "edgy" ranks right up there with "twerk," "yummy," and "ridonkulous" on my list of least favorite words). One investor left me a strange late-night voice mail and then apologized for it on the phone the next day. "Sorry about that," he said. "I was all messed up on Percocet and Jack Daniels." I'd be freaked out if a friend said something like that, so needless to say, I did not go with that firm.

It seemed most of the venture capitalists I met with had recently and unanimously "discovered" that women liked to buy things online. They were super-stoked on the idea of a female-run business that sold things to women. I happened to check a lot of the boxes that they were excited about at the time, but they had no idea why Nasty Gal was special. It was obvious to me that their ideas weren't their own. One person asked to call my former COO, Frank, to talk about the business. I said sure, and gave him Frank's number. I later found out that he asked if I had a "spending problem." When I heard this, I thought to myself, *Dude: I built a multimillion-dollar business out of $50 and no debt—does it look like I have a spending problem?*

The only person I liked was Danny Rimer. Danny's company, Index Ventures, was based in Europe and had just opened their U.S. office far from Silicon Valley, in San Francisco's SoMa neighborhood, where the start-ups were. Danny had also already been investing in great fashion companies since before the other guys knew what fashion was— like ASOS and Net-a-Porter—so I knew that he was interested in Nasty Gal because he truly got us, not because we were the hot ticket. Danny had a brand—and I get brands. Index has chosen to surround itself with the best entrepreneurs and the best companies. I realized that, just as all department stores are not created equal, all investors are not created equal. Danny was my flagship Barneys.

After our first meeting, Danny called me and said, "You have a community. I get it." And I knew it was a match made in heaven. He also seemed to inherently understand the challenges we were facing. At this point in time, we still didn't have a head of finance, so we couldn't answer half of the questions other firms were asking us. Danny recognized this. He didn't ask us to go through due diligence (a term for digging through the company's receipts and financials). Realizing that I'd never used PowerPoint, Danny also had an associate from his team put together an investment deck for me to present to the partnership. When it came time to negotiate, it was like haggling at the flea market. He said, "I would like to buy X percentage of the company for X amount of dollars," and I said, "No, X percentage for Y dollars." And then we were done. It was a small investment—$9 million is not a small sum, I know—but it is atypical for a company of Nasty Gal's size. Yet I was new at this and Danny knew it. Instead, he leaned in and suggested we shake hands on doing something small now with the goal of doing another, bigger investment if we both still liked each other in six months.

Had I not found Danny, I probably wouldn't have taken investment. But his contrarian way of thinking, as well as his instant understanding of what I was building, made me love him. Index passes on investments that a lot of these guys drool over. I liked that. For Index, investing in a business is not just a mercenary transaction. Index wants to be involved and they want you to be exciting. They've passed on good financial investments because they simply didn't like the entrepreneur. And I respect them for that.

What I really learned from this entire experience is that people want to invest in businesses that don't need money, and that your ability to execute has to be just as strong if not stronger, than your idea. And, just like how I want to buy that item behind the counter at the vintage store that isn't for sale, venture capitalists want to invest in businesses that also "aren't for sale." Human nature tells us to want what we can't have. A desperate business is not a good look, and most investors won't touch that with a ten-foot pole.

Even if you have no plans to ever find yourself sitting

across from a venture capitalist with a pitch in your hand, getting this far in #GIRLBOSS training should have taught you to rule nothing out. Perhaps someday you will have a business that's the next big thing (I hope you do!), so it doesn't hurt to be prepared. Here are a few tips for sparring with investors that you can also apply to other areas of your life.

Turn-ons:

Good people: This is the number one thing that distinguishes one start-up from another. Investors, like employers, look for people who are excited about what they're doing and have the integrity to keep their promises. They also want to see that you have a smart, creative team with diverse experience. The concept of "good people" should apply to every part of life. Surround yourself with people who are engaged, honest, and confident enough on their own quest to support you on yours. There is no time for losers.

Scalability: Ultimately, the market, technology, fashion—whatever it is that is at the core of your business— is going to change, so investors as well as employers need to know you'll be able to change with it. Or even better: Stay ahead of it. Most investors are looking to make a return of at least five to ten times what they invest, so you have to demonstrate that your company can achieve that growth.

Evidence of demand: Have something that a lot of people are going to want. By the time I was talking to Index, we already had hundreds of thousands of rowdy Nasty Gals the world over, so it was very easy for us to prove that there was a more than viable market for our brand. When you're applying for jobs, it's best to be employed while doing it. You want the world to know that you're not lollygagging between gigs, but instead have a lot of choices in front of you and are actively charting your own path.

Outside validation: You can sell yourself all day long, but sometimes it's more effective when other people sell you (aka your references). An investor is much more likely to be interested in your pitch if he or she has already heard about you because people are excited about what you're doing. Great references (or a glowing introduction) never hurt.

Uniqueness: This is where it comes down to your idea and how good it is. Taking someone else's idea and adapting it for a different demographic isn't really an idea, so good luck finding someone to invest in Nasty-Guy.com, your idea for a site that sells badass clothing to dudes. In whatever you do, you're not going to stand out unless you think big and have ideas that are truly original. That comes from tapping into your own creativity, not obsessing over what everyone else is doing.

Turnoffs:

Overconfidence: You need to be passionate and excited about what you're doing, but don't be so blinded by it that you're unrealistic. If you're saying things like "No one has ever done this before," it usually just comes across as cocky or, worse, uninformed. As a #GIRLBOSS you should always be confident—and absolutely sure—about what you know, but humble about what you don't.

Talking about how soon you plan to exit: This might work for some people, but most investors are in it for the long haul. It's for the same reasons that I don't like it when I ask people where they want to be in two years and they answer that they want to own their own fashion business. People like to see evidence of commitment.

Typos and general unpreparedness: Yeah, this is just basically a turnoff for anyone, everywhere.

PORTRAIT OF A #GIRLBOSS:

Jenné Lombardo, Founder of the Terminal Presents; theterminalpresents.com (@JenneLombardo)

I get my hustle on every day. For me it's family first, paper second. Growing up, I always wanted to have my own office—I thought that epitomized success. I also always wanted something that was mine. Something that was tangible, which I could look at and say, with pride, "I did this."

When I was growing up my family lost a lot of our money and I was forced to go get it on my own. My work ethic is partly fear-driven—I never want to be without financial stability again. Also, I want to be on Fortune's "40 Under 40" list. (I'm too old to make Forbes's "30 Under 30"!) I feel like I take risks every day, and the biggest risk I take is on life. Without risk there is no reward and no change. How boring would this world be if there weren't people out there like Rosa Parks, Richard Branson, Bill Gates, and Steve Jobs? There are two types of people out there—those who do and those who don't. If you are a risk taker, you have to feel comfortable in knowing you could fail. You have to have enough confidence and conviction to go full force even if things don't work out. For us risk takers it's an occupational hazard. If we fail, we get right up and try again. Just doing is reward enough.

I am creative in almost every aspect of my life, particularly when it comes to solving problems. Whether we chose to believe this or not, there is a solution to everything. It's all a matter of perspective and how willing we are to be flexible when it comes to our point of view. I don't see things the way a trained eye would. In fact I question everything—how can I make this better, how could we be operating at maximum efficiency? It's a blessing and a curse. Challenging convention and not accepting the norm is a world I have come to live in. I read everything and I ask a lot of questions. You won't get anywhere just talking about yourself. Listen. It's one of the greatest gifts you could give to yourself.

I'm constantly inspired by everyone I work with and the tribes we assemble. I am inspired by youth culture. I love knowing everything—what they are wearing, what they are listening to, what apps they are using. Kids are the future. If I wanna stick with the future, I gotta stay close to the game.

My advice to #GIRLBOSSes is: Create your own job. Become the master of what you do. Fully immerse yourself in your culture. Be humble: You are never above having to pack boxes. Never forget where you came from. And always be polite. Good old-fashioned manners can get you very far.

OWN YOUR
STYLE
LIKE
YOU OWN
YOUR USED
CAR

10

Creativity in Everything

Every child is an artist.
The problem is staying an artist
when you grow up.

—*Pablo Picasso*

At age three I was a speaker. When music played through our living room stereo, I stood in the corner like a statue with my mouth open, pretending the sound was coming out of me. At age four I was a camera. I took pictures with my eyes. I framed my photo within my vision and blinked my eyes to snap the shutter of my memory. Since that time I've been impersonating inanimate objects at every opportunity. But don't call me a wallflower.

Early experiments in selfie photography and top hats.

My creativity began to crystallize as a teenager, when I got my first camera. At age eighteen I got hit by a car while riding a borrowed bike to dumpster-dive for bagels. That sucked but I got enough settlement money out of it to take myself to Portugal and Spain (I spent the rest on an electric guitar). It was on this trip that I became obsessed with seeing the world through a lens—and returned home with more excitement than ever for photography.

Armed to Bless

A picture is a secret about a secret, the more it tells you the less you know.

—*Diane Arbus*

Soon after my trip abroad, I enrolled in full-time photography classes at City College of San Francisco, where I learned to develop my own negatives and expose my own prints. For our final project we had to shoot a series of some sort, and I decided on a Russian Orthodox Church down the street from my apartment. The building was tiny, and from the outside you could hardly tell it was a church at all. It was the architectural equivalent of a loner.

I felt a kinship to this humble outsider church in the middle of San Francisco's metropolis, so I knocked on the door and asked Mother Maria, the nun who lived there, if I could take some pictures. I grew up Greek Orthodox and still have an appreciation for the sights, sounds, and scents of the faith, which I think helped gain Mother Maria's trust. It turned out that she hadn't grown up Orthodox but had chosen the faith. My conversations with her were pretty powerful—I knew so many people who had dropped out of society in so many ways, but here was a woman who had looked the world in the face and decided, in the purest way possible, that she wanted none of it.

Mother Maria was a badass.

The Russian Orthodox faith eschews any sort of luxury, which means the entire service is spent standing. In Mother Maria's view, the world outside the church—which she called the "worldly world"—was a place full of gluttonous distractions that kept us from discovering our true spiritual selves. She invited my worldly self in nonetheless, allowing me to photograph her and the church. The photos didn't turn out that great; I still had a lot to learn.

205

A few weeks later, though, Mother Maria called me. The old priest had died and she wanted me to photograph his funeral. When I arrived his body was near the altar in a simple casket handmade from a few pieces of wood with a white satin sheet stapled to the interior. Aside from me there were about eight other people in attendance. So many of the worlds that I had dipped into played at shrugging off modern society, but the priest was a man who had truly rejected it. In a city full of noise, he'd found light by living in the shadows. Holy shit, is that heavy.

My baptism by fire helped me to find comfort in many different environments. I photographed truckers, bartenders, and outsiders in Nowheresville. I had begun to feel like I really knew what I was doing with a camera. And I'd upgraded to my twenty-first-birthday gift, a Hasselblad medium-format camera. That camera, to this day, is the best gift I've ever been given. It was my mother's last effort to help me find my way. I decided that I wanted to attend the San Francisco Art Institute. In order to do so, I needed to have a finished photography portfolio.

In order to fulfill this prerequisite, I chose to return to the church. Mother Maria introduced me to a priest, Brother Eugene, who lived on a small plot of land outside Santa Rosa, selling his vegetables at the farmers market on weekends. I spent the day with him and we talked about everything under the sun. He fed me trailermade borscht and I went on my way. I then set off to a Russian Orthodox monastery in Point Reyes.

The monastery was one of the most beautiful places I have ever been. There was a shipping container where a young monk spent his days dipping beeswax candles to be used in churches and sold in gift shops. Some men built caskets. Some gardened. They were shut off from the world but they were open enough to let me in. I couldn't help but think that when they weren't wearing robes, I could have mistaken these guys for metalheads.

In the end I decided that I couldn't stomach the $50,000-a-year tuition and chose to forgo art school. But my series, which I called *Armed to Bless*, was an education in itself: It was one of the first times that I had ever finished something that I set out to do.

Find Your Framework

Applying to SFAI gave me the framework to be free within a set of rules in a way that school and jobs had not allowed me. *Armed to Bless* was an accomplishment beyond just taking pictures. It taught me that when I do things because I want to do them, and not because I have to, I can accomplish a lot. This type of framework is all around us and it also exists outside applying to or attending school. When it came to starting my own business, I found the framework that I needed on eBay. I probably could not have built a website of my own at that point, but my ambition grew with each crack of opportunity. The framework of eBay presented me with a series of easy-to-complete tasks (take photo, upload photo, write description) that eventually added up to a business. Starting it was as easy as picking a name and uploading the first auction. That instant gratification would never have come had my first step been to write a business plan. And without that instant gratification I might not have kept going. If you're dreaming big, #GIRLBOSS, don't be discouraged if you have to start small. It worked for me.

Putting the "Art" in Sandwich Artist

Curiosity about life in all of its aspects, I think, is still the secret of great creative people.

—*Leo Burnett*

Anything you do can be creative. If, when you make a smoothie, you try to make the best smoothie the world has ever tasted, it's a creative act. If you throw a frozen banana and some yogurt in a blender and hit puree, well, not only is it uncreative and boring, but I also feel really bad for you.

I was always looking for ways to make my job creative, no matter what that job was. At Subway I loved the giant spray nozzle that hung above the dishwashing sink. Blasting mayo off of the spatula was uniquely satisfying. I liked making bread, spacing out the little twisted sticks of dough into perfect patterns on trays before sliding them into the oven. I learned the secret to the perfect doughy center in Subway's cookies: slamming the tray down on the counter, causing the cookies to spread out while the pan was still hot. And any job that pays you for slamming things . . . well, consider yourself lucky.

None of the jobs at Nasty Gal are shitty to me, and I know because at some point I've done almost all of them. Whether it was styling, directing models, steaming clothing, or shipping an order—they were all creative. And when something got really boring, I turned it into a game to see how quickly, efficiently, and accurately I could get the job done.

The Venn Diagram of Creativity and Business

> Access to talented and creative people is to modern business what access to coal and iron ore was to steelmaking.
>
> —*Richard Florida, author of* The Rise of the Creative Class

I would never have accomplished what I have had I felt forced to choose between my creative talent and my business acumen. At Nasty Gal, I'm the CEO and creative director, two titles that are rarely on the same business card—but what no one seems to talk about is that business *is* creative. I'm as creative when I'm choosing an investor as when I'm reviewing collection samples. I have as much fun hiring people as I did with a camera in my hand.

Keeping the Nasty Gal brand consistent as we have grown has been one of the biggest challenges I've faced. I've gone from being a solo artist to one part of a killer band. Our C-level team is the rhythm section, the rest of the team is playing guitar and keys, and I'm just scatting. *Be-bop a doo-wa* . . .

It wasn't too long after I'd launched the eBay store that I started to recognize how important the thumbnail photos were. Thumbnail photos are prime real estate in e-commerce—they hook your customers in while simultaneously informing them about what they're looking at. These thumbnails can't be too messy or too bland. They must display the items clearly so that as prospective customers zoom quickly through the catalog page, they know what they're looking at and also find it interesting. I saw that when the shape and style of an item was clearly visible in even the tiniest photo, it inevitably went for a higher price than a thumbnail where the silhouette was obscured or confusing to look at.

To this day I blur my eyes when I edit photos. I load all my photos on Bridge, shrink them down super-small, then cross my eyes like a goofball and flag the images that still catch my eye. This allows me to edit quickly without getting distracted by the details—if the composition or silhouette sucks, it doesn't matter what the model's face says. The DNA of a successful image, and brand, must be encrypted into its tiniest representation while gracefully telling the same story in its largest incarnation. My thumbnail photos were the postage stamps to Nasty Gal's success.

I was used to making dozens of little creative decisions every day, but designing the first Nasty Gal website was my first macro "branding" project. Though once again, I didn't see it as a branding project—Nasty Gal just needed a website, so I made one. I had no formal graphic design training, but knew what I liked and what I didn't, and had spent so much time observing and talking to my customers—through eBay and MySpace—that I was confident I knew what would appeal to them.

Block type was really big in 2008, so I found some clunky font on a German graphic designer's blog and downloaded it for free. I smashed the letters together, making one solid shape, and the first Nasty Gal logo was created. I went through a million iterations of the site, but it was always a fairly simple design. The color scheme was always pink, black, and gray because I didn't want it to be too heavy. I used a close-up shot of my friend Dee's face in the navigation (Dee was an early eBay model and now works for Nasty Gal as an apparel designer) and it was up there for years. The main tenets of the navigation were "Shop New" and "Shop Vintage." It's not as if I invented the English language here, but Nasty Gal was definitely one of the first websites to sell both new and vintage and position it as such.

I knew how to use Photoshop from editing photos, but I did not know how to use InDesign, so I designed Nasty Gal's first website entirely via Photoshop. Also, as I was self-taught, I didn't know any shortcuts. I moved everything one pixel at a time. I must have spent hours hitting the arrow key, like *doo doo doo doo doo doo doo doo doo doo doo doo doo doo doo doo* . . . okay, now that box is halfway to where I want it to be, so . . . *doo doo doo doo doo doo doo doo* . . . You get the picture. When Cody, who helped with the site development, showed me that I could hold down the shift key and move something like ten pixels at a time, it was as if the heavens opened up, the angels sang, and I got back several hours, maybe even days, of my life.

I have always been an observer. When I see music live, I like watching not only the band but the crowd as well. What are their favorite songs? Who's a fan and who has never even heard this band? Where's the obligatory fifty-five-year-old man with no rhythm who arrived alone and is louder than anyone else in the room? Currently, I am always trying to imagine things from the customer's point of view. Now that Nasty Gal's creative decisions are made by our creative team, they have to look at things from three views: their own, the customer's, and mine. Thank God I hire brave people, because the inside of my head can be pretty weird sometimes.

Nasty Gal is now at an inflection point where we have to institutionalize the magic, as I like to say. That means that everyone's job, to some extent, is to pull out of my head what has made Nasty Gal successful for the past seven years. When the brand was an extension of just me, I never had to stop and ask myself whether or not it was "on brand." Today, our team is constantly working together to examine what has made us successful, what of that we want to keep around, and what newness we can introduce to evolve the brand. We then have to communicate that and share it. Our creative team is learning how to think like I think and I'm learning how to think like they think. Brains everywhere, all the time. Cue air drums.

PORTRAIT OF A #GIRLBOSS:

Leandra Medine, Manrepeller.com and author of *Seeking Love, Finding Overalls*

When I was a kid I really thought I was going to be a ballerina, but then I realized I suck at dancing. So by the time I was in college, I wanted to become a reporter. I hoped I'd get a fact-checking job at New York magazine out of college, but instead I started Man Repeller.

I was a junior at the time and started the blog because I was writing so much content that was not funny at all and I just felt like I needed a place to inject a little bit of humor. What I wanted to do with my life figured itself out. I did not by any stretch of the imagination think that it was possible to take my blog any where that professional stuff happens. Sometimes I still feel like the universe is playing a trick on me. Since 2010, I have since grown Man Repeller from a one-person blog (here's hoping, fingers crossed) to a website with staff writers and graphic designers and ad sales people and bikini waxers on demand! Just kidding. Fuck waxing.

I remember when I was younger that every time my mom wanted to buy something expensive, she had to run the purchase by my dad. I knew I never wanted to have to ask anyone to appease my indulgences, so that was a point of motivation to work hard. If you're working, you're working hard, and if you're not doing that, what are you doing? I also think you age a lot quicker if you can't keep yourself busy and under the right, healthy dose of stress. Too much of anything obviously isn't good, but as my dad always said: Overwhelmingly busy is a much better state to be in than overwhelmingly bored.

Fashion has always informed the way I approach life. It's also helped me manipulate my moods: I could be having a shitty day but the right pair of shoes can sometimes change that—which is powerful. I make a lot of jokes about fashion, but I love it. And on the topic of style, I think clothing will always look good—no matter how outlandish or ridiculous you might think it is—if you wholeheartedly own it. If you feel equally as excited and comfortable in a fruit-silhouette head contraption as you do in a pair of jeans, the rest of the world will watch. And likely in admiration. There are no apologies necessary for being you.

It sounds incredibly platitudinal, but no one will

ever be able to love you if you don't love yourself. What's beautiful about it is that if you love yourself enough, you don't need the validation from anyone else. My advice to #GIRLBOSSes is to get excited about the mistakes you'll make.

Own Your Style Like You Own Your Used Car

When you don't dress like everyone else, you don't have to think like everyone else.

—Iris Apfel

As much as I would like to say that photography was my first love, I think my first real creative effort was getting dressed.

Both my parents were well attired, but my mom especially had great style. Before she headed out the door, she put the finishing touch on her outfit by "punking" (better

Mom, and me, with her "punked" collar. 1987.

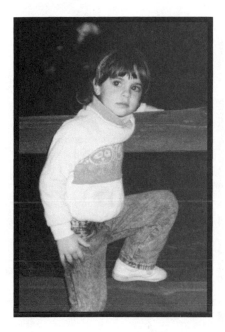

Before I knew that real punks don't wear polo shirts.

known as popping) the collar of her '80s polo shirts. It was always in my blood to care about what I wore and how it fit. At age six, my one true love was a pair of acid-wash jeans with an elastic waist. In sixth grade I became obsessed with the Sanrio crew: Hello Kitty, Pachacco, Kero Kero Keroppi, and the lot. My look could best (or worst?) be described as suburban mall Harajuku girl through a Northern California lens: baby T-shirts, barrettes, and white Walgreens' knee-high socks that I wore with my Converse One-Star sneakers.

When I was fifteen I liked a pair of bedraggled brown Levi's corduroys that I found at the Salvation Army by my house so much that I wore them at least five days a week, until they met their untimely demise in a gas station parking

A staple look from my boring-ass Abercrombie phase. 1998.

lot (I'll spare you the gory details, but let's just say that it involved a really upset stomach, lack of a nearby public bathroom, and me crying in shame). Even when I was in my Abercrombie & Fitch phase (yes, even I have succumbed to peer pressure), I washed my jeans after every wear so that they still fit exactly the same as they did when I bought them.

I was a '90s teenager, so of course I went through a grunge phase, donning bell-bottom flares that dragged on the ground and an equally shapeless men's V-neck sweater. My clothing choices were in line with my contrarian nature. As

I mentioned earlier, my mom begged and pleaded with me to buy clothes at the mall, a typical teenage girl's dream; we spent hours there only to leave empty-handed as store after store failed to usurp my preference for the corduroy and threadbare T-shirts I could only find at the local thrift store.

After that, I went through a couple of different iterations of skater girl: the cute type, with tiny board shorts, a tight tank top, and skate shoes; and the not-so-cute type, when I cut off all my hair and paired those skate shoes with baggy Dickie's work pants.

At age seventeen I was a crust punk who refused to change her all-black clothes. At eighteen I was goth, which still involved all-black clothes, but at least now I changed them. That was when I lived in Seattle—and the goth suited the gloom. After that, when I moved back to San Francisco, I became a rock 'n' roller and that stuck for a long time. I hooked my thumbs through my belt loops and did honky-tonk scoots across dance floors. My long hair parted in the middle and I wore exclusively vintage T-shirts with high-waist jeans that practically grazed my boobs.

I've always been willing to throw *myself* at the wall and see if *I* stuck when it came to general life experiences, and my approach to my personal style hasn't been any different. I was always willing to try something new. As soon as I was over it, I moved on. And *thank God* I moved on. The whole pick-a-decade thing doesn't really age well—you get to a certain point where it just ages you. Your style is a representation of who you are, and trying to pick your identity as an adult (anime? cowboy? new age?) is just not a good look. I think that now, depending on my hair, I dress closer to my Tim Burton–character roots than I have been in a long time—and I'm comfortably rock 'n' roll with a disco soul.

W&H Instead of T&A: The Nasty Gal Look

Even though Nasty Gal is still in adolescence, when it comes to trends we've already been through many phases. This isn't because we've been trying to figure out who we were, but because evolution is the name of the game when you're in the fashion industry. And we don't just want to stay on top of that game—we want to stay ahead of it. We want to lap our competitors and leave them in our dust.

Christina and I always did this by shopping with a focus group in our heads. At trade shows we held up different pieces and asked each other, "Can you see anyone in the office wearing this?" The office has always been populated with girls who are style-obsessed and Nasty Gals IRL, so if the answer was no, we just didn't buy it. I remember in 2009 we bought a whole lot of all-black everything. Rick Owens and Alexander Wang ruled the runways; under their influence girls were obsessed with asymmetrical draping and lug-soled combat boots in black black black. If anything was adorned with metal studs, then it was almost too hot to handle. If we sold studded underwear, I'm sure it would have flown off the site. By the time girls could walk into Forever 21 and snap up studded booty shorts and platforms, we figured it was time to lay off the studs. This was about the time when the fashion world started to get a little preppier. Our customers loved short sets, button-up pinafore shirts, and ice-cream pastel colors, so for a while that was what we sold before we inevitably moved on to something else.

We always listen to what our customers want, but we don't buy into every trend that comes along. If the silhouette du jour suddenly becomes that of the Stay Puft Marshmallow Man and fashion tells you that you should be wearing egg-shaped sweatshirt dresses that obscure your waist and emphasize your butt, well, you can buy that someplace else. Nasty Gal doesn't want you to look like a marshmallow.

Selling vintage is a really good exercise in learning to recognize what people want right now as well as what they'll always want. Nasty Gal always participates in the dialogue of the fashion industry, but there are core things that we talk about even if they're not gracing the pages of *Vogue* at that particular moment: a rock tee, a motorcycle jacket, red lipstick, biker boots, skinny jeans, leather pants, a white lace dress. You have to know what looks good on you personally, and we have to know what looks good on us as a brand.

The epitome of style has always been the chic French woman: an Alexa Chung–looking gamine with simple, elegant clothes, such as loose shift dresses, and an overall effortless, understated cool. Yet if I may quote Bob Dylan, "it ain't me babe." I've got hips, and as soon as I got to a point in my life when I started to dress according to what actually suited me, I realized that if I didn't wear something that accentuated my waist, I looked like I was toddling down the street in a refrigerator box.

When I started the eBay store, my only styling experience was getting dressed in the morning, so I dressed the models as though I was dressing myself. That meant that if a garment didn't have a waist, I gave it one. I also learned that while hints of androgyny worked for my favorite models, it didn't work on eBay, where the thumbnail photo was pretty much the size of, well, a thumbnail. Thus, if my models had short hair, or even long hair pulled back into a ponytail, they might as well have had shaved heads. We always went with a look that was either a strong lip or a strong eye, which is now a staple of the Nasty Gal look. My most iconic model was Nida. A towering Thai girl at five foot nine, she was as bold as they came. She did her own hair extensions and wore false eyelashes as part of her everyday routine. In the photos she looked like a bombshell with hair down to her waist. This really stood out on eBay, where most of the models at the time were still dress forms or hippies in sandals. From this amalgamation of things the Nasty Gal look was born. For us, it's never been about boobs and butts, but waists and hips (W&H instead of T&A . . . Get it?) and the styles that show them off: high-rise pants, cropped jackets, fit and flare, bandage dresses. Nasty Gal shows a little bit of skin somewhere—like a thigh-high slit in a maxi skirt—and if it's not, it's making up for it with a whole lot of attitude. I believe a #GIRLBOSS should have a sneer and a smile in her back pocket, ready to whip either out at any moment.

Nasty Gal has always paired vintage pieces with modern styling. Anyone who's spent some time in thrift stores understands that part of wearing vintage is to know that you can't always expect it to come right off the rack looking perfect. You must be able to see past that sad sack dress on a plastic hanger with a price tag stapled to it and imagine the myriad things you can do with it. I've belted muumuus, hacked hems, and rolled sleeves on the regs, and learned that sometimes the perfect oversized sweater or shrunken jacket is only as far away as the men's aisle or children's section. On eBay I sold a lot of children's coats because, when they were styled right, they looked like the perfect cropped jacket. One of my own favorite pieces of vintage is a light pink child's peacoat that looks straight off a Marc Jacobs runway. Eventually, I got to a point where I'd dressed so many models that I could look at something on a hanger and know exactly how it would fit on a girl. I could even look at a model and know what her measurements were and all of this helped make me a good buyer because it helped Nasty Gal avoid stocking stuff that was cute in theory but awkward when you put it on.

Despite the fact that I'm wearing YSL platforms as I write this, I have always believed that it shouldn't cost a lot of money to look good. When Christina and I started buying new brands, we experimented with some more expensive offerings, and $300 dresses simply didn't sell. Our customer works hard for her money, so it goes without saying that she's going to be careful with how she spends it. That also highlights the difference between fashion and style: You can have a ton of money and buy yourself all the designer goods you can stuff into the trunk of your Mercedes-Benz, but no amount of money can buy you style. Having good style takes thought, creativity, confidence, self-awareness, even some-times a little bit of work. And there you have it, folks: A little bit of skin + attention to silhouette + an attitude + a vintage piece or two + a decent price tag = Hello, Nasty Gal.

It's Not Hot. It's Not Cold. It's Cool.

I like to say that Nasty Gal is dressing girls for the best years of their lives whether a girl is eighteen, twenty-five, thirty-five, or sixty. At a recent meeting, when several of us were locked away in a war room, strategizing for the future, some-one asked an assistant if it would be difficult for her to relate to me if I were older. "No," she replied, "Sophia's a badass bitch and she'll always be a badass bitch!" That I've man-aged to build a company where an assistant feels comfort-able calling the CEO a badass bitch in a room full of senior executives is pretty amazing.

The heartbeat of Nasty Gal doesn't exist in one style, trend, or article of clothing. It's in the way we talk, the way we carry ourselves, and the way we see the world. If you scroll through Nasty Gal photos from the early days, this is obvious: The styles have changed, but the attitude is the same. The Nasty Gal look has always been that hard-to-nail-down, you-know-it-when-you-see-it quality; the ultimate babe who's one-third girl-next-door, one-third genius, and one-third party monster. She's cool. It's this combination that has made casting models especially challenging for us—it's not enough that a girl is tall, gorgeous, and fits the clothing—she has to be cool on top of it.

My definition of what's cool may be a rare one. It's not about being popular, or waking up with a pizza spinning on the turntable like an '80s teen movie. Being mean won't make you cool, being rich won't make you cool, and having the right clothes, while it may help, won't make you cool. It's cool to be kind. It's cool to be weird. It's cool to be honest and to be secure with yourself. Cool is the girl at a party who strikes up a conversation with you when she notices you don't seem to know many people there. It's that vibe that I always wanted Nasty Gal models to have. I want our customer to look at Nasty Gal and see someone who could be her friend modeling the clothes. Or even better, I want her to project herself into the lifestyle and attitude, soaking it up to add to her arsenal of amazing qualities of which having great clothes is only one small part.

Own Your Style

The last thing I'd ever subscribe to are fashion rules. However, I do think that you should put effort into what you wear. Clothing is ultimately the suit of armor in which we battle the world. When you choose your clothing right, it feels good. And there's nothing shallow about feeling good. Owning your style, however, is much more about your attitude than it is about what's on your back. But don't underestimate the transformational possibilities that getting dressed can afford you.

While I have the freedom to wear whatever I want at work, I dress the part. In fact, everyone at Nasty Gal does. When I'm confident in what I am wearing, it makes me feel more confident throughout the day. Granted, I could probably negotiate a deal in my pajamas, but I'm a lot more dangerous in a pair of leather pants and boots that could hurt a fool.

Some girls can pull off a trend as though they just rolled out of bed, grabbed the first thing they saw, and skipped out the door without even giving the mirror a sideways glance. When I try to wear too much of a trend, I end up looking the opposite—like I spent way too much time in front of the mirror. It's important to know which trends are for you and which ones you should watch walk down the runway and right on by.

We've all seen girls who constantly tug at the hem of their dress, readjust straps, and mess with their hair. If you're not confident, no dress, no matter how smoking-hot it is, will solve that problem for you. If I see you in a club hobbling like an injured baby colt, I want to push you over. I *will* push you over. And, if I can push you over, you're not owning anything; and that's what I want you to do, #GIRLBOSS: Own your style like you own your used car. This means wearing what you like and what makes you feel good. And it means getting dressed for yourself—not your boyfriend, not your friends, not your parents. Here's one thing the fashion industry probably won't tell you: Confidence is more attractive than anything you could put on your body.

And that brings me to my other point: Owning your style sometimes takes effort, and it's okay to expend effort on how you look. For a long time women wore only dresses and spent hours on their hair because that is what society mandated. But now we don't have to do it—we *get* to do it. Being a girl is fun. We can experiment with our look as much as we want. I remember being a little girl and watching with fascination as my mom used an eyelash curler. The key is making sure you're doing what you want, not doing things because your boyfriend can't stand to look at you without any makeup on. If every other girl you know is wearing a push-up bra and you do not want to wear a push-up bra, then by all means, do not wear one. But they're there if you need 'em.

There are certain common themes that I hear when I talk to Nasty Gal customers all over the world. "I was the only girl who didn't shop at the mall," a lot of them say. "My town was so boring that just putting effort into my look was seen as crazy." And to that, I always say, "Hell yes." Putting in effort is exactly what you should be doing. You should get dressed for your life. I don't care if the only place you have to go is the post office: Get dressed, #GIRLBOSS, and let your freak flag fly.

PORTRAIT OF A #GIRLBOSS:

Ashley Glorioso, Senior Stylist at Nasty Gal

When I was younger, I hated being in school. I hated everything about it, so I knew that whatever I did wasn't going to involve any extra schooling past high school—I couldn't get out of that place fast enough. I thought I was going to work with animals, but then realized I was too emotionally attached to them, so needed to work with something that couldn't get hurt or die. Clothes. Perfect!

I've been pedal to the medal ever since and I have no intention of stopping! I started working retail in high school to earn some cash of my own, and I realized that there was so much to the retail world. I worked for small boutiques at first, and for pennies, but learned so much about the industry that it made my time there priceless. I worked at a small store in Westlake Village, California; I was only sixteen but running the store. I was comfortable being in charge at such a young age. Baby boss lady!

I learned about everything from merchandising to receiving, and even made sure I learned about stuff that I wasn't even interested in. I felt as if the more I learned about retail, the more options I would have later on. I think it's good to have more than one skill set in the fashion industry. A lot of companies require you to wear many different hats, so the more experience you can gain, the better!

I started styling for fun on a friend's lookbook shoot when I was eighteen, and thought, *Wait, I like this! And I'm decent at it!* I was shocked people did this for work. That was when I started to pay way more attention to what was going on in fashion—delving into every season of shows and every magazine I could get my hands on. I studied the makeup artists, the hairstylists, the photographers, the clothing stylists . . . I learned how everyone had a different eye, and how it was all art.

I think fashion is the ever-undulating industry, and style is something that a person has inherently without really trying. I went through so many weird phases throughout my life. I was never a great vintage shopper, but now I am well versed in the magic of a good tailor, so I don't hesitate to buy vintage because I know that I can rework that baby into utter perfection. Nowadays my style is all over the place and I try not to fit into any one category. Some days I feel very gypsy and wear a long skirt with a weird top, a long vest, a furry vest over that, and 2,056 necklaces and rings. Other days I wear my boyfriend's ripped T-shirt and some huge jeans and do not give two fucks. Sometimes I wear a frilly dress with socks and Mary Janes, and other times a suit. So be it. I like to keep people guessing. Hell, keep me guessing!

Above anything, I think clothes should make you feel good about yourself! I can't imagine anything worse than a girl trying to fit into a certain trend and then feeling uncomfortable with what she's wearing. What's the point!? Who cares if everyone is wearing boyfriend jeans? If you feel like a chunky dude with poopy pants, take them off! You should walk out of the house and be thinking, Damn, I look good.

I'm super lucky that I can do what I love every day, so that keeps my creative juices flowin' like wine. I also keep myself busy with freelance projects on the weekends so I never feel as if I'm not creating something. Sometimes I need a creative break, so I lie on my couch for hours at a time watching Law & Order: Special Victims Unit. This usually happens after I have styling dreams where I keep saying "cute" over and over again.

I never assisted anyone; I just gave it my all. I always networked with anyone whom I met in the industry, I believed that I could do it, and people believed me. *Get your hustle on.* My uncle always instilled the importance of work ethic in me from a young age. I asked for things and he always said, "If you want something, you have to earnnnnn it!" I thought it was the most annoying statement ever. Yet the older I got, the more I realized I could get a job, make my own money, and not have to ask for things. So I did. And it was so satisfying!

Obviously, the older I got, it wasn't just about buying things, but not wanting to be the girl living paycheck to paycheck, as in, "Can I pay my rent this month?" I wanted to live comfortably and not be stressed about finances. I also wanted to be able to do nice things for my family. I knew that they appreciated even the small things, like my being able to pick up the tab at dinner. The more I accomplish in life, the more I realize that I am not a complete and utter failure, and I'm actually proud of myself! I had no idea what I wanted to do out of high school, so to be where I am now . . . that's somethin'.

11 The Chances

Dreams are today's answers to
tomorrow's questions.

—Edgar Cayce

W hat are the chances?

That's a good question.

More than a half-million new businesses are started per month in the United States alone, but 80 percent of them will fail within the first year and a half. So what are the chances that mine would still be alive and thriving seven years later? You could do some calculations, plot some graphs, and determine the exact probability, but I think we all agree by now that that's not my jam! The answer, no matter how you spin it, is that the chances were that of a snowball in hell.

I have a tattoo that reads "1%." It's something I got years ago with Gary when he was already my ex, but it was our humorous homage to the ideals of the one-percenters. In the wake of a bunch of bad press, the American Motorcyclist Association once claimed that 99 percent of its members were regular citizens and only 1 percent were outlaws. The gnarliest of the gnarly outlaw bikers latched on to that, calling themselves one-percenters. While we weren't outlaws, Gary and I identified with their ethos that when you are a one-percenter, you live your life your way. Currently, the popular meaning of the so-called 1 percent refers to Wall Street, and that ethos is completely different. This idiomatic shift has become especially ironic for me, but the tattoo hasn't lost any of its significance. It's a reminder of how unlikely it was that I'd ever find myself seated in the corner office.

In a 2011 *TED Talk* in San Francisco, author and speaker Mel Robbins talked about how the chances that you are you are about 1 in 400 trillion. (Yes, that's a four hundred followed by twelve zeros.) This takes into account the chance of your parents meeting out of all the people on the planet, the chance of them reproducing, the chance of you being born at the exact moment that you were, and every other wildly improbable factor that goes into each individual person. The whole point of her crazy calculation was that we should take the sheer improbability of our own existence as a kick in the butt to get out of bed in the morning. If you hear this fact as discouraging—that you're only one in billions—then flip the script. You are one in billions! Someone has to succeed, so it might as well be you.

I didn't stick around high school long enough to be voted "Most Likely to" anything, especially since my Subway polo, Dickies, and I looked about as far away from Most Likely to Succeed as you could possibly get. Anyone looking for a sure bet, in business or in life, would never have put their money on me. But that didn't dissuade me from betting on myself. In the end I beat the odds. Now, whenever I'm faced with improbable situations, I remind myself that if I really want something badly enough, I have it within myself to make it happen.

My entire path is littered with my defying every piece of advice I've ever been given. I'm giving you carte blanche to pick and choose from the advice outlined in this book. Hell, ignore it all if you want. But don't ignore this: You create the world, blink by blink. It is entirely yours to discover and yours to create.

That's the number one thing, perhaps even the only thing, you can absolutely count on. Regardless of what your dreams are, if you listen only to those around you, the chances of your dreams coming true are very small. The world loves to tell you how difficult things are, and the world's not exaggerating. And that's a real bummer. But, here's the real shit: You can't have it all, and nothing comes easy. You will make sacrifices and compromises, get let down and let other people down, fail and start over, break some hearts, take some names, and learn to pick up and continue when your own heart gets broken. But difficult doesn't mean impossible, and out of the bajillions of things in this universe that you can't control, what you *can* control is how hard you try, and if or when to pack it in.

Paul recently reminded me of a Nasty Gal barbecue when, unprompted, he took the hose and began to spray me with water. I grabbed the nearest thing I could—a hamburger patty—and threw it square at his chest, knocking the wind out of him. He was wearing a white shirt, and it left a big meat stain right on the front. So when life hits you with something unexpected, you have to be prepared to hit right back—and leave your own smear in the process.

In a now famous commencement speech at Stanford University, Steve Jobs urged the graduating class to "stay hungry. Stay foolish." Never let go of your appetite to go after new ideas, new experiences, and new adventures. Compete with yourself, not with others. Judge yourself on what is your personal best and you'll accomplish more than you could ever have imagined. Life stops for no one, so keep moving. Stay awake and stay alive. There's no AutoCorrect in life—think before texting the universe. Breaking the rules just for fun is too easy—the real challenge lies in perfecting the art of knowing which rules to accept and which to rewrite. The more you experiment, take risks, and make mistakes, the better you'll know yourself, the better you'll know the world, and the more focused you'll be.

And once you've found success, don't stop. It's not about being insatiable; it's about not resting on your laurels. This crazy, loopy universe that we live in is pretty entertaining, and we're only here for a short amount of time. #GIRLBOSSes make it count. Look up and look around, and if you're not finding something inspiring, then you're probably not looking hard enough. Remember, I touched every piece of clothing in those thrift stores. You have to do that with your life.

An advantage of being naïve is being able to believe in oneself when no one else will. I was dumb enough and stubborn enough to pour everything I had into a business called Nasty Gal and to tune out people who tried to tell me I was doing it wrong. Had I stopped at the first catty eBay seller who tried to crush my spirit, I'd probably still be peddling shoes that I'd never be able to afford to wear. If you start listening, you should find that your heart has known what's up all along.

This short life of mine thus far has been a pretty fantastic ride, there's no doubt about that. I'm resolved to making sure that doesn't change anytime soon. When I think about the future, I know that the most fantastic things are too awesome to even imagine today. Great entrepreneurs are like Indiana Jones: They take leaps before seeing the bridge because they know that if they don't, someone else will get that holy grail. That holy grail is yours for the taking.

Bad bitches are taking over the world. When I walk into the Nasty Gal offices, it's clear: Busting your butt isn't just for the wallflowers anymore. We've arrived, and we're killing it.

There's a chance for you, #GIRLBOSS. So take it.

ACKNOWLEDGMENTS

Thank you to my mother, for putting up with the years of heartbreak that I wreaked upon her. To my dad, for teaching me to negotiate like a mobster and for creating in me the self-critic who keeps me honest. To Christina Ferrucci, my sister from another mister. To Yia Yia, for buying me books with titles such as *Odd Jobs for Kids* and *Liking Myself*. To Gary Mancillas, for knowing me; to Kate Stewart, for letting me crash; and to Joel Jarek DeGraff, for putting up with the war room that made this book possible. And to Donna Summer, the poodle that continues to teach me that there is a God.

Also, a big thank-you to Kerri Kolen and Maria Gagliano, my amazing editors at Putnam and Portfolio, who pulled the depth from my depths. To Andy McNicol, for knowing I "had a book in me" from day one, and to "Scary" Gary Stiffelman, for having my back. To Kelly Bush, for taking a chance on me. And to Kate Williams, for being my Ritalin throughout the writing of this book.